THE CRISIS IN PLANNING
VOLUME TWO
The Experience

THE
CRISIS IN PLANNING

Volume Two
THE EXPERIENCE

Edited by

MIKE FABER
AND
DUDLEY SEERS

Published by

CHATTO & WINDUS
FOR
SUSSEX UNIVERSITY PRESS

1972

Published by
Chatto & Windus Ltd.
40 William IV Street
London W.C.2

*

Clarke, Irwin & Co. Ltd.
Toronto

ISBN 0 85621 003 X

Printed in Great Britain by
T. and A. Constable Ltd.
Edinburgh

CONTENTS

CONTENTS · VOLUME ONE

LIST OF PARTICIPANTS†

Conference Chairman:

Gamani Corea, *Permanent Secretary, Ministry of Planning and Economic Affairs, Ceylon.*

Participants who chaired plenary discussions and study groups:

John Adler *Director, Programming and Budgeting Department, International Bank for Reconstruction and Development.*

Miss Peter Ady *Fellow of St Anne's College, Oxford.*

Austen Albu, M.P. *House of Commons; formerly Minister of State for Economic Affairs.*

A. A. Ayida *Permanent Secretary, Ministry of Economic Development, Nigeria.*

Lord Balogh *Fellow of Balliol College, Oxford.*

C. P. Cacho *Bursar, University of the West Indies, St Augustine; formerly Economic Secretary, Ministry of Finance and Economic Development, British Honduras.*

Gamani Corea *Permanent Secretary, Ministry of Planning and Economic Affairs, Ceylon.*

Hollis B. Chenery★ *Professor of Economics, and Director, Project for Quantitative Research in Economic Development, University of Harvard.*

William Demas *Economic Adviser to the Prime Minister of Trinidad.*

Harry Hanson *Professor of Politics, University of Leeds.*

Branko Horvat★★ *Director, Yugoslav Institute of Economic Sciences.*

Gaston Leduc *Member of the French Institute; Professor of Development Economics, University of Paris*

Athole Mackintosh *Director, Overseas Development Group, University of East Anglia.*

Ambassador Edwin Martin *Chairman, Development Assistance Committee, OECD.*

Hon. V. S. Musakanya★ *Minister of State for Technical Education and Vocational Training, Zambia.*

C. D. Msuya *Principal Secretary, Ministry of Economic Affairs and Development Planning, Tanzania.*

Señora Ifigenia de Navarrete *Director, National School of Economics, City University, Mexico.*

Felipe Pazos *Consultant, Office of the Program Adviser, Inter-American Development Bank.*

R. S. Porter *Director-General of Economic Planning, ODM.*

Hans Singer *Fellow, IDS,*

Arnost Tauber★★ *Institute of International Politics and Economics, Prague.*

Maurice Zinkin *Head of Economics and Statistics Department, Unilever.*

† Contributors of main or supplementary papers are shown by ★ for Vol. I and ★★ for Vol. II. The positions listed here are as they were at the time of the Conference, 1969.

Participants who introduced plenary discussions:

A. L. Adu *Deputy Secretary-General, Commonwealth Secretariat.*

Samir Amin *Professor of Economics, Dakar.*

Lord Balogh *Fellow of Balliol College, Oxford.*

William Demas *Economic Adviser to the Prime Minister of Trinidad.*

Okon Eshiett *General Secretary, Nigerian Union of Commercial, Technical and Allied Employees.*

Tilak Gooneratne *Deputy Secretary-General, Commonwealth Secretariat.*

Harry Hanson *Professor of Politics, University of Leeds.*

Colin Leys★ IDS *and Professor of Government, University College, Nairobi.*

Michael Lipton★★ *Fellow,* IDS.

W. J. M. Mackenzie *Professor of Government, University of Glasgow.*

B. S. Minhas★★ *Indian Statistical Institute.*

Brian Reddaway *Director of the Department of Applied Economics, University of Cambridge.*

Dudley Seers★ *Director,* IDS.

Gueorgui Skorov *Institute of World Economy and International Affairs, Moscow; formerly with* IIEP, UNESCO, *Paris.*

Speakers at special sessions:

G. R. Aithnard *Personal Assistant to the President, African Development Bank.*

Lord Blackett F.R.S. *President of the Royal Society.*

Asa Briggs *Vice-Chancellor, University of Sussex.*

Mrs Helen Hope (formerly Lady Cohen) *Ariel Foundation.*

Bruno Knall *South Asia Institute, University of Heidelberg.*

C. D. Msuya *Principal Secretary, Ministry of Economic Affairs and Development Planning, Tanzania.*

A. E. Oram, M.P. *Parliamentary Secretary,* ODM.

Felipe Pazos *Consultant, Office of the Program Adviser, Inter-American Development Bank.*

P. S. Narayan Prasad★★ *Director, Asian Institute for Economic Development and Planning.*

Rt. Hon. Reginald Prentice, J.P., M.P. *Minister of Overseas Development.*

Dudley Seers *Director,* IDS.

Sir Geoffrey Wilson *Permanent Secretary,* ODM.

Participants acting as secretaries of study groups and rapporteurs:

Brian Van Arkadie★★ *Fellow,* IDS; *formerly Economic Adviser, Ministry of Economic Affairs and Development Planning, Tanzania.*

Raymond Apthorpe *Visiting Fellow,* IDS.

Clive Bell *Fellow,* IDS.

Robert Cassen *Lecturer in Economics,* LSE.

Charles Cooper *Fellow,* IDS; *and Senior Research Fellow, Science Policy Research Unit, University of Sussex.*

Michael Faber *Overseas Development Group, University of East Anglia.*

Keith Griffin** *Fellow of Magdalen College, Oxford.*

A. G. Hurrell *Head, West and North Africa Department,* ODM.

Richard Jolly *Fellow,* IDS.

Leonard Joy *Deputy Director,* IDS.

Michael Lipton *Fellow,* IDS.

Señora Ifigenia de Navarrete *Director, National School of Economics, City University, Mexico.*

Charles Shackleton *Research Officer,* IDS.

Hans Singer *Fellow,* IDS.

Martin Staniland *Fellow,* IDS.

Paul Streeten *Warden, Queen Elizabeth House, and Director, Institute of Commonwealth Studies, Oxford.*

Other participants (not already listed):

Peter Abelson *Research Staff, Roskill Commission.*

S. M. A. Adam *Central Planning Organisation, Saudi Arabia.*

H. Anguiano *Office of Economic Advisers, Ministry of Presidency, Mexico.*

Miss Winifred Armstrong *American Metal Climax Inc.*

A. T. Baillee *Financial Policy and Aid Department, Foreign and Commonwealth Office.*

Z. H. K. Bigirwenkya *Secretary-General, East African Community.*

E. Boeninger** *Director of the Bureau of Budget, Chile, and Dean of the Faculty of Economics, University of Chile.*

Frank Bogdasavich *Director, Canadian University Service Overseas.*

Tse Chun Chang *Assistant Director, Centre for Development Planning, Projection and Policies, United Nations, New York.*

Pramit Chaudhuri *Lecturer in Economics, University of Sussex.*

Ronald Dore *Fellow-elect,* IDS, *and Professor of Sociology,* LSE *and* SOAS.

Dharam Ghai** *The Institute for Development Studies, Nairobi, and staff member, Commission on International Development (Pearson Commission).*

Oscar Gish *Research Fellow, Science Policy Research Unit, University of Sussex.*

Reginald Green *The Treasury, Tanzania.*

G. K. Helleiner *Professor of Economics, University of Toronto.*

Dudley Jackson *Department of Applied Economics, University of Cambridge.*

Emanuel de Kadt *Lecturer in Sociology,* LSE, *and Fellow-elect* IDS.

J. King Gordon *Assistant Director, Centre of International Cooperation, University of Ottawa.*

John Knapp *Lecturer in Economics, University of Manchester.*

François Le Guay *Director, Industrial Policies and Programming Division,* UNIDO; *formerly of the French Commissariat du Plan.*

Ben Lewis *The Ford Foundation.*

Miss L. G. Lewis *Assistant to the Agricultural Adviser, Barclays Bank,* DCO.

Arthur Livingstone *Professor-elect and Head, Department of Overseas Administrative Studies, University of Manchester.*

Lazlo Lukacs *Visiting Research Professor, Nigerian Institute of Social and Economic Research, University of Ibadan, and Hungarian Academy of Sciences.*

P. C. Mahalanobis *Indian Statistical Institute, Calcutta.*

A. Mahmood *Trade Promotion Study Group, Commonwealth Secretariat.*

C. J. Martin *Adviser on Planning Organisation, Development Services Department,* IBRD.

A. R. Abdel Meguid* *Project Manager,* UNDP *Planning Project, Ceylon; formerly Director of the Aswan High Dam Project, United Arab Republic.*

Donald Mills *Director of Planning, Jamaica; on loan to Government of Bahamas as Permanent Secretary, Ministry of Planning.*

A. El Morshidy *Acting Director, The National Planning Institute, Cairo.*

Ajit Mozoomdar *Minister, Indian High Commission.*

H. M. A. Onitiri *Director, Nigerian Institute of Social and Economic Research, University of Ibadan.*

Roger Opie** *New College, University of Oxford; formerly Senior Economic Adviser, U.K. Department of Economic Affairs.*

P. G. Ottewill *Science, Technology and Medical Department,* ODM.

Gustav F. Papanek* *Director, Development Advisory Service, Centre for International Affairs, Harvard University.*

Colin Rosser *Visiting Fellow,* IDS; *formerly Chief Consultant, Ford Foundation Advisory Group, Calcutta.*

Edward Rubin *Deputy Managing Director, Litton-Greece.*

E. Ratna Sabapathy *University of Birmingham.*

Robert D. H. Sallery *Director of Planning, Canadian University Service Overseas.*

Bernard Schaffer *Fellow,* IDS.

Tom Soper *Director of Studies,* ODI.

Osvaldo Sunkel** *Institute of International Studies, University of Chile.*

Richard Symonds *Fellow,* IDS.

Jan Tinbergen *Adviser to various governments and international organisations. Nobel prize-winner in Economics. Director, Netherlands Economic Institute and Professor of Economics, Rotterdam University.*

H. A. Turner* *Burton Professor of Industrial Relations, Faculty of Economics and Politics, University of Cambridge.*

Jan Vrany *Institute of International Politics and Economics, Prague.*

Albert Waterston* *Lecturer, Economic Development Institute,* IBRD.

Participants attending individual sessions (not already listed):

D. W. Berk *Economic Planning Staff,* ODM.

Mrs Felicity Bolton *Summer Schools on Problems of World Order.*

F. N. Brockett *East Africa Department,* ODM.

G. A. Bridger *Economic Planning, Geographical Division,* ODM.

R. G. Dyson *Deputy Chairman, Barclays,* D.C.O.

George Foggon *Overseas Labour Adviser, Foreign and Commonwealth Office and* ODM.

D. E. Glason *Development Administration and Training Department*, ODM.

Raymond Goldsmith *Professor of Economics, Yale.*

Terence Higgins M.P. *House of Commons.*

His Excellency Dr Nai Sunthorn Hongladoram *The Ambassador of Thailand.*

P. H. Johnston *Development Administration and Training Department,* ODM.

Neville Kanakaratne *Ceylon High Commission.*

A. J. Killick *Economic Planning Staff,* ODM.

James Mark *Under Secretary,* ODM.

I. T. Nance *Development Administration and Training Department,* ODM.

Geoffrey Oldham *Senior Research Fellow, Science Policy Research Unit, University of Sussex.*

C. D. Powell *Planning Staff, Foreign and Commonwealth Office.*

A. M. Turner *Head, Development Administration and Training Department,* ODM.

The Rt. Hon. Eric Williams, M.P.* *Prime Minister of Trinidad.*

Howard Wriggins *Director, Southern Asia Institute, Columbia University, New York.*

ACKNOWLEDGEMENT

The Editors would like to thank Barry Peters and Susan Purdie Peters of the Institute of Development Studies for their work in helping to prepare these volumes for publication.

SOME ABBREVIATIONS USED

ADB	Asian Development Bank
CECLA	Comisión Especial de Coordinación Latino-Americano
CMEA	Council of Mutual Economic Aid
COMECON	Council for Mutual Economic Assistance
DC	Developed Country
ECAFE	Economic Commission for Asia and the Far East
ECLA	Economic Commission for Latin America
IBRD	International Bank for Reconstruction and Development
ICORS	Incremental Capital Output Ratios
IIEP	International Institute for Educational Planning
LAFTA	Latin American Free Trade Association
LDC	Less Developed Country
ODM	UK Ministry of Overseas Department (now Overseas Development Administration)
NSS	National Sample Survey
UNCTAD	UN Conference on Trade and Development
UNRISD	UN Research Institute for Social Development

INTRODUCTION

THIS volume contains three types of papers. There are accounts of the machinery and process of plan preparation in seven different countries including, in some cases, a review of how such machinery evolved. There are edited resumés of the critical discussions which followed the presentation of these descriptive papers. And there are two papers which, in respect of the Indian sub-continent and of Latin America, explicitly address themselves to analysing what went wrong with the planning process and to 'planning the improvement of planning'.

What we have called the main descriptive papers (although all of them contain elements of appraisal and criticism as well) were prepared specifically for, but in advance of, the Crisis in Planning Conference that was held by the Institute of Development Studies at the University of Sussex in the summer of 1969. They were intended to provide a factual framework of 'case studies' to complement the papers on principles and general problems which have been collected together in Volume One. The other two types of contributions evolved from the proceedings of the Conference itself.

Our introduction to Volume One referred to two of the main shifts of emphasis which are obviously being manifested in the whole world-wide process of planning. One of these is a shift away from the preparation of vast plan documents towards greater concern with plan implementation; another is a lowering of the priority given to economic growth as against other social objectives. Other lines of association or division appeared at the Conference – less clear but of equal interest – and are reflected in these papers. Thus the political scientists and the practical men of finance at one stage combined to charge the economic planners with ignoring the reality of political decision making, with concentrating too much of their time on unrealizable medium-term macro-plans at the expense of sector programmes and realistic annual budgeting, with 'being happier with figures than with people' and with 'a tendency to see themselves as demiurges'. (But it was noticeable that the leading practical politician present, Eric Williams of Trinidad, did not associate himself with these charges.) A calmer accusation was that although economic analysis needs to be comprehensive, it did not always follow that planning ought to be.

There was some divergence of view as to whether there really was a crisis in planning (was it not rather a question of 'planning in a crisis'?), but general accord that it was certainly an appropriate occasion for self-criticism amongst planners. That planning has given rise to numerous disappointments; and that it has mainly (too mainly?) been the preserve of the economists (and of insufficiently practical economists at that) seemed to be propositions that were generally accepted. However, collective self-criticism itself turned out to be a term capable of ambiguous interpretation – should it mean criticism of 'my own' performance or that of colleagues working in the same field? 'I detect an interesting declension at work,' Lord Balogh at one point remarked, 'I plan, you pseudo plan, he does not plan at all'.

Editing conference papers is an austere business. Much of the cut and quip of discussion vanishes beneath the mark of the blue pencil; most of the camaraderie – if such gets recorded at all – disappears between the scissors' blades. Our own favourite short story was contributed by Branko Horvat. When he had asked a colleague what was the main instrument to ensure plan implementation in Yugoslavia, the reply, after a pause, had been 'the telephone'. In a sense – that of enabling planners to learn from the experience of others – we should like this volume to be regarded as an instrument too, selectively employable for 'planning the improvement of planning'.

ASIA

Chapter One

OBJECTIVES AND POLICY FRAME OF THE FOURTH INDIAN PLAN

An Appraisal

DR B. S. MINHAS

FOR a decade and a half India ran a bold, new experiment in national planning. It was bold in the sense that a poor, agrarian economy was expected to be transformed into a self-generating, modern economy in a period of twenty-five to thirty years; and new because the experiment was to be conducted in the context of a democratic, federal system of representative government.

OBJECTIVES AND STRATEGY OF PLANNING IN THE NEHRU ERA

The basic premise of India's Five-Year Plans, particularly of the Second and the Third Plan, was 'development along socialist lines to secure rapid economic growth and expansion of employment, reduction of disparities in income and wealth, prevention of concentration of economic power and creation of the values and attitudes of a free and equal society'.

A few of the salient operative elements of this strategy are worth highlighting:

(1) Aside from a programme of land reform and ceiling legislation which was in various stages of implementation, no basic alteration in property relations was envisaged. In other words, the objectives of 'reduction of disparities in income and wealth' and 'prevention of concentration of economic power' were sought to be achieved not through redistribution of property and wealth, but through other means.

(2) A self-generating economy, capable of fast and self-sustained growth, was to be ushered in by 'building of economic and social overheads, exploration and development of minerals and promotion of basic

industries like steel, machine building, coal and heavy chemicals'. The rapid expansion of an *efficiently* operated public sector was expected to (i) remove basic deficiencies in economic structure, (ii) generate substantial surpluses for its continued growth and (iii) reduce the scope for accumulation of wealth and large incomes in private hands.

(3) The private sector of the mixed economy in India was to function 'within the framework of national planning and in harmony with its overall aims'. Any accentuation in tendencies towards concentration of economic power in this sector was to be countered by widening opportunities for new entrants and for medium and small-sized units and through effective exercise of Government's powers. The size difficulties of small producers in industry and agriculture were to be overcome by organizing them on co-operative lines.

(4) A fast and concentrated development of education and other social services was to be an important means for ensuring greater equality of opportunity. Scheduled tribes and castes and other backward classes were to receive favoured treatment under special programmes.

(5) To help create 'the values and attitudes of a free and equal society', a process of democratic decentralization was started. The spread of the community development movement and the creation of panchayati raj institutions in rural areas were to help this process.

This, in brief, was the strategy of planning which appeared to be in operation during the Second and Third Five-Year Plans. In spite of a number of references in the Plans to the employment problem, the creation of employment opportunities was seen more or less as an adjunct to or a by-product of the development strategy outlined above.[1] India did follow this strategy of planning and achieved notable success in a number of areas. However, the failures of Indian planning have been glaring enough to have pretty nearly succeeded in pushing its successes into insignificance. National planning in India has been on the run for a number of years. Its complete withering away was strongly hoped for in many quarters. Nonetheless, long-term national planning is now being revived in India and the occasion warrants a scrutiny of our planning experience.

[1] Except in the Second Plan where the conflict between the objective of self-sustained long-term growth and immediate increase in employment opportunities was sought to be resolved by a policy of encouraging labour-intensive techniques in consumer goods industries even as the capital-intensive sector of heavy industry was being expanded rapidly. Nonetheless, no success in this regard was achieved during the Second Plan period.

GADGIL ON PRE-GADGIL PLANNING

One such scrutiny was provided by an eminent critic of Indian planning, Professor D. R. Gadgil, in December 1966.[1] He gave an able documentation of its achievements, and I can do no better than repeat, in a summary form, his assessment of the positive side of the ledger of Indian planning. He noted that 'successes have been in the field of public investment in irrigation, power, transport, etc. and in basic industries and to some extent in the extension and diversification of educational and health services. The other notable success has been in the creation of a diversified industrial complement in the private sector.' The efforts in the field of 'agricultural production' and 'in raising the level of taxation and in gathering resources in public hands' were rated by him in the category of 'partial success'. Professor Gadgil summed up his assessment of planning as follows: 'In short where the Government of India directly undertakes large programmes of public expenditure it succeeds best. It fails to the extent that the planned use of resources lies in other hands. . . .'

On the negative side, Professor Gadgil noted the following failures:

(i) the failure of the tax system 'as means of restraining consumption and of promoting equality';

(ii) the failure of rural industrialization and the consequent accentuation of employment problem;

(iii) the complete failure to evolve a properly structured, overall regulatory framework for the private sector.

It was this 'total absence of a policy frame' which was 'the most outstanding feature of the planned Indian economy'. The net result of all this, according to Professor Gadgil, was 'that in the aggregate the economy operates as almost a *laissez faire* economy, in part modified by the operation of particular controls'. All the failure of planning – the stagnation of exports, *ad hoc* import regulation, inefficiency and rising costs, devaluation of the rupee in 1966, the increasing dependence on foreign aid, instability of prices, accentuation of inequalities, etc. – was attributable to the absence of an integrated policy and overall regulatory frame.

---

[1] See D. R. Gadgil, 'Planning Without a Policy Frame', *Economic and Political Weekly*, Annual Number, February 1967.

POLITICAL AND ECONOMIC SETTING OF THE FOURTH PLAN

This was an important assessment of Indian planning. The time was December of 1966: Professor Gadgil was giving his views on the Draft Fourth Five-Year Plan, which, shortly after, was to be aborted.

India had been without a current plan for two years running when efforts for the revival of planning were resumed. The first step in this direction was the reconstruction of the Planning Commission. None of the authors of the abandoned Fourth Five-Year Plan was taken into the reconstituted Commission. Its membership was altogether new. Professor D. R. Gadgil, old critic and keen analyst of India planning, was brought in to lead this Commission and the future course of planned national development. The new Commission were expected to review past trends in development, reorganize the planning effort, appraise the operational significance of changes in the political, social and economic situation for national planning, redefine the objectives and strategy of planning, and prepare a programme of medium- and long-term development to achieve the chosen objectives. Nobody expected this task to be easy. There was a serious recession in industry. Prices were rising at a fast rate. A growing trade deficit, mounting debt obligations, a very strained foreign exchange situation and extreme shortfalls in agricultural production were other characteristics of the situation. And above all, planning had lost a good deal of political support.

It was against this unenviable constellation of circumstances that the new Commission were to seize and elaborate a strategy of planning and put forth a programme. Their labours are now embodied in the Fourth Five-Year Plan–Draft, 1969-74. All students of Indian planning, in their appraisal of this Document, will need to keep firmly in mind the setting in which planning has been resumed.

AIMS AND OBJECTIVES OF PLANNING IN THE FOURTH PLAN

All talk about a policy frame without reference to a well defined set of objectives, towards the achievement of which this policy frame is to be directed, is empty of content. The objectives of Indian planning from mid-fifties to mid-sixties were clearly stated. The strategy of approach towards these objectives was also clear. The salient elements of this strategy are listed in the beginning of this paper. Professor Gadgil's charge was that Indian planning during the Second and Third Plans lacked a well articulated regulatory policy frame. To a large extent this was a fair charge.

Social and Economic Democracy or Socialism?

In its statement of the aims and objectives of planning, however, the Draft Fourth Plan has taken a rather ambivalent position.

One definition of objectives runs as follows: 'The broad objectives of planning could thus be defined as rapid economic development accompanied by continuous progress towards equality and social justice and the establishment of a social and economic democracy'.

Rapid economic development and progress towards equality and social justice were also among the objectives of Indian planning in the past. However, the older objective of a 'Socialistic Pattern of Society' or 'development along socialist lines' has now been interpreted as 'the establishment of a social and economic democracy'. What exactly is the meaning of 'social and economic democracy'? Does this change merely represent an interchange of phrases with the same meaning? Or, does it mean an alteration in the concept of Indian 'Socialism'? The term 'Socialistic Pattern of Society' did have an accepted, even if vague, meaning. But what does 'economic democracy' mean? In affluent countries, where abysmal want has been eliminated, economic democracy has a meaning almost synonymous with a free market economy: one unit of purchasing power is one economic vote. The Planning Commission seem to intend a broader definition which includes the availability of opportunities for education, public health and sanitation, drinking water supply, etc., for large masses of people irrespective of whether they are rich or poor. In other words, the Planning Commission envisage a complement of 'socialised consumption', which would be available to all sections of society and they propose that special emphasis should be placed 'on the common man, the weaker sections, and the less privileged'.

INDIAN SOCIALISM IN PRACTICE

It is often claimed that in the Fourth Plan Draft the old objective of establishing a 'Socialistic Pattern of Society' has been watered down. This charge is difficult to prove or deny. Let us, however, try to see what Indian socialism has turned out to mean in practice. The socialistic intentions of independent India were pitted against the outmoded attitudes of a strongly feudal and caste- and status-conscious society, which has been unwilling to accept the rigorous code of private as well as public behaviour implied in the concept of socialism.

Whether it was the operation of public sector enterprises, or the construction of infra-structure facilities in the field of irrigation, flood control, power, transport, etc., or the operation of a licensing system for control of investments and imports, or the distribution of food and fertilizers etc., the basic fact of *the distribution of public largesse to the not-so-poor* was ever present. We built temples of modern industry which were overcapitalized. Elaborate townships were provided and included in the capital charges and economic rents were never charged. Sound pricing policies for the products of these industries were shunned. Huge dams, flood control, irrigation and power facilities were built with public funds, but the collection of development levies and the charging of proper irrigation rates and power tariffs were forgotten. Food and fertilizers were distributed at prices below costs. Most of these benefits accrued to the relatively well-to-do. A number of public inducements have been responsible for a great spurt of luxurious, private residential construction in big cities; whereas nothing significant has been done to improve the living conditions in the sprawling slums. The operation of the licensing system, and the licensing of imports in particular, instead of checking concentration of wealth and countering inequalities, have resulted in the creation of huge illicit private gains (these would run into hundreds of crores of rupees) which have remained outside the scope of taxation. All of those programmes were introduced in the name of a 'Socialistic Pattern of Society'.

The characterisation of Indian 'Socialism' outlined above was a product of the genius of a people for whom the government had, for all practical purposes, always meant something alien to the society that it governed. Deliberate cheating of government in the matter of tax dues, stealing of materials from government construction works, blatant use of public office for strictly personal ends, and evasion of public responsibility in general are the other manifestations of the same basic attitude of our people towards government. The persistence of this attitude towards government in independent India is the most glaring failure of the process of political and social education.

PROSPECTS FOR A SOCIAL DEMOCRACY IN INDIA

Among other things, the establishment of a 'social democracy' has now been made an explicit aim of Indian planning. The chances of success do not look good. To find evidence for inegalitarian attitudes one does not have to search far. Right inside of Yojana Bhavan, where programmes for the establishment of a social democracy are being framed, one is struck with the prevalence of contrary attitudes. Luxurious, air-conditioned comfort is the monopoly of high civil servants and their bosses; whereas secretarial staff in adjacent rooms have to bang cold fingers on their typewriters in winter and smudge away sheets of paper in the sweltering heat of May and June. It is true that the government of a poor country cannot provide full comfort to all its employees; nevertheless, in the distribution of such comforts, a complete disregard of the functional efficiency of this distribution is indefensible. As one moves away from men of significance, which means moving vertically up beyond the second to the third, fourth and fifth floors of Yojana Bhavan, one is struck with the sharp decline in standards of sanitation and other amenities. One is not sure whether charity begins at home; but social democracy certainly does not seem to.

In private industry and finance such inegalitarian attitudes are a legend; but at least one does not come across many pretensions to the contrary. Caste and class loyalties are strong and the politicians exploit them for their narrow ends. These are the attitudes on which a programme for establishing a social democracy will have to be anchored. In the absence of a clear programme of direct action to fight these attitudes and tendencies, the aim of establishing a social democracy in India is not something that economic planning alone can tackle. Whatever progress towards 'social democracy' the Fourth Plan might achieve, will accrue more or less as an adjunct to the overall programme, very much like the employment opportunities in the Second and Third Plans.

GENERAL APPROACH TO THE FOURTH PLAN

On the basis of experience since the beginning of the Third Five-Year Plan, the Planning Commission have drawn two important lessons for 'framing a correct approach to the Fourth Plan':

(1) A need 'to adopt measures which will maintain relatively stable conditions while development proceeds' has been recognized. The concept of stability is seen to consist of measures to assure stable food prices and the eschewing of inflationary methods of financing the development effort.

(2) Another important lesson is the recognition of 'the need to take quick strides towards self-reliance'. The concept of self-reliance is interpreted to mean progressive reduction of net aid and the specific target is that 'foreign aid net of debt charges and interest payments will be reduced to about half by the end of the Fourth Plan compared to the current levels'.

It is also recognized by the Commission that the current tempo of development is insufficient to bring about significant improvement in living standards of the people. However, the continuity of even this moderate rate of growth is seen 'to be threatened if instability emerges because of weakness on the food front and too great a dependence on foreign aid'.

By and large, the size and pattern of investment outlays in the Fourth Plan seem to have been derived from three crucial sets of numbers:

(1) Agricultural output is expected to grow at the rate of 5 per cent per year;

(2) Export growth of 7 per cent per annum is expected;

(3) Compared to the current levels, net aid will be reduced to about half by 1974.

The consistency of all other calculations seems to hinge on these three pre-targets or numerical assumptions.

PROSPECTS FOR AGRICULTURAL PRODUCTION

Between 1951 and 1965, agricultural output had grown at 3·10 per cent per annum; 1·40 percentage points of this growth were the contribution of gross crop area expansion, 1·33 percentage points were due to productivity rise and the remainder was accounted for by changes in the composition of output due to crop pattern changes. Leaving the abnormal crop year 1965-66 out of reckoning, the comparison of trends in these components between the period covered by the first two Plans and the first four years of the Third Plan may be used for speculating about the possibilities of agricultural growth during 1969-74. During the two periods mentioned above, trend growth rates of agricultural production were not significantly different, though the point estimate for the trend rate of growth in the period 1951-61 was 3·58 per cent and only 3·0 per cent in the later four-year period (1961-65). Growth rates in productivity, though not different in a statistical sense, were 1·5 per cent and 2·5 per cent respectively in the first ten-year and later four-year periods. The later period growth rate in productivity had a large standard error around it and was not significantly different from zero. However the story on area expansions was significantly different in the two periods. From a very significant growth of 1·8 per cent a year during the first ten years, the growth rate in output attributable to area expansion had come down to an insignificant 0·12 per cent. Unlike the fifties, we were not able to ride high on the crest of gross crop area expansion in the early sixties. The net sown area expansion in India slowed down sharply and the rate of growth of double cropped area did not pick up appreciably in the sixties.

A step up in the growth rate of agriculture from around 3·1 per cent in the period 1951-65 to 5 per cent in 1969-74 would have to come from (i) a very distinct increase in the rate of increase in double-cropped area, and (ii) sharp increases in productivity per gross crop acre. For both of these things to happen in adequate measure, Indian agriculture would have to put in tremendous effort in irrigation, scientific soil and water management, plant nutrition and improvement of the genetic capabilities of crops. There are some hopeful signs in these areas.

Apart from extension of irrigation facilities and applications of scientific soil and water management methods, sharper increases in double cropping are very much dependent upon the introduction of selective mechanisation and the development of varieties of crops whose planting could be staggered to overcome the shortages of labour and draft power which occur in peak seasons. Unfortunately the question of power constraints on agricultural development has not been seriously looked into by agricultural planners. Even more important than the investment aspect is the question of the availability of relevant information about the power, water, soil nutrition and organizational requirements of programmes for increasing double-cropping in specific areas. Our lack of such information is only too apparent and our knowledge of soil-water-plant relationships is nominal. The long-term possibilities of agricultural growth are by no means meagre; but with our present knowledge, a near doubling of the rate of increase of the rate of growth in productivity per acre, which is implied in a jump in overall agricultural growth from 3·1 per cent per year during 1951-65 to 5 per cent a year during a short span of five years 1969-74, does not look like a realistic possibility.

The foodgrains part of agricultural production in the Fourth Plan is of crucial relevance. Assuming that the 1968-69 production of foodgrains is no larger than in 1967-68, the target of 129 million tonnes in 1974 implies a growth rate of 6·18 per cent per year. This looks very ambitious. Between 1950-51 and 1964-65, foodgrains production expanded at a rate of 3·21 per cent per year, cereals at 3·41 per cent, pulses at 1·67 per cent. During the same period rice output grew at 3·63 per cent. The two years, 1965-66 and 1966-67, that followed were extremely abnormal. But 1967-68 was a year of good harvest. Yet even in 1967-68 the output of foodgrains as a whole, of all cereals, of rice as well as pulses, was below the relevant trend levels. The output of foodgrains, for instance, was about two million tonnes less than the expected trend level estimate based on observations from 1950-51 to 1964-65 and 1966-68. The only exception was wheat. A good bit of this extra output of wheat over and above the trend estimate is attributable to increase in area under wheat compared to 1964-65 levels. Approximately 1·4 million tonnes out of a total wheat output of about 16·5 million tonnes in 1967-68 could be attributed to changes in the technology of wheat production, and wheat production has further increased in 1968-69. But this solid achievement in wheat is not matched by other cereals and pulses.

In spite of the continuous chatter about the Green Revolution as a *fait accompli*, the fact is that in 1967-68 and in 1968-69 the actual foodgrains output has been below the corresponding estimates based on past trends. The trend level estimate of foodgrains output in 1968-69, for instance, works out to about 100·5 million tonnes. Taking this estimate as the base level for the Fourth Plan, the target of 129 million tonnes in 1974 implies a trend rate of growth of approximately 5 per cent per year. Can this be achieved during the Fourth Plan? Can the old trend rate of foodgrains growth, which was between 3·1 to 3·2 per cent per year, be replaced by a 5 per cent trend rate of growth? In spite of our good progress in wheat production, such a large gain is unlikely.

POLICY FRAME FOR AGRICULTURAL PRODUCTION

Size of Production Unit in Agriculture

The Planning Commission seem to be in favour of a clear separation between the objective of equity in landholding and economic efficiency. It is their hope that the ceiling legislation would achieve equity in some measure. They note, however, that there is a clear trend 'towards reduction in size of the average holdings'; but they consider that in India 'the basic problem is *not* that of bringing about large redistribution of land surface but that of combining land surfaces operated by vast numbers of small-holders into units suitable for efficient cultivation' (p. 26). A reconciliation of this conflict between private ownership of land and efficient organization of production has always been sought in co-operative farming on voluntary lines. This policy has failed to produce any results. The Planning Commission in their turn have noted this failure; but probably for want of better things to suggest, the Commission go on to say that 'except for continuing the present schemes of encouragement to co-operative farming it has not been possible to propose any additional programmes in this Plan'.

The question, whether the Planning Commission are serious in their support of co-operative farming or not, is only of academic interest. The case for economies of large-scale production in Indian agriculture has not so far been proved; the fact that co-operative farming has not been able to gain a foothold would itself seem to suggest that economies of scale are not overwhelmingly large. Irrespective of the existence or non-existence of scale economies, however, the questions of ownership and efficient operation of land are intertwined. The desirability of a programme of land redistribution cannot simply be wished away by asserting that land redistribution is *not* our 'basic problem'. If, in the interest of institutional stability, current Indian polity demands that property relationships in agriculture should not be disturbed, then the only honest thing to do is to record it as a premise of planning.

Research and Extension

The crucial role of public agencies in organizing the passing on of the results of research was recognized quite early. In recognition of the need for integrating research, teaching, and extension, nine agricultural universities came to be established in the sixties on the pattern of American land grant colleges. The Fourth Plan proposes to strengthen and stabilize these institutions and contemplates establishing four new universities of this type. The Planning Commission intend 'to evolve a system of tying up of the disciplines of research in collaboration with one another and develop a system of feedback through extension'. In order to do this efficiently, the Commission should prepare an inventory of important questions for agricultural research and see to it that research data flow back into the planning process at all levels. Critical analyses and use of such data would point up the need for further research, and in this manner, the Planning Commission could give a purposeful direction to further agricultural research. After nearly twenty years of planning, we still do not have adequate and meaningful data for preparing agricultural programmes and plans; without doubt, efforts to get the right kind of agricultural research data generated would pay handsome dividends.

Price Policy for Agriculture

In the Fourth Plan a vigorous price policy is envisaged to ensure an allocation of land among crops which will be in accordance with the targets laid down in the Plan. Control over crop patterns will have to be exercised but, according to the Commission, this control will be exercised only through the manipulation of an otherwise stable structure of relative prices. The Planning Commission seem to regard non-price variables to be either ineffective or unnecessary for the control of crop patterns. It is quite true that within the overall constraints of soil and climatic conditions in an area, a comprehensive price policy can influence crop patterns in the desired direction and that the use of non-price instruments may be quite unnecessary for controlling crop patterns. Nonetheless it is worth noting that some non-price instruments, such as timing of water deliveries from reservoir systems, can be put to effective use for inducing crop pattern changes. In some situations they can be even more effective than prices. We should not deny ourselves the use of such instruments of policy but rather use them wherever they can be used efficiently.

Seeing the need for evolving a comprehensive structure of relative prices and manipulating it for achieving the desired mix of outputs is one thing, but to construct such a structure is quite another matter. The analytical and informational requirements of an operational policy exercise of this nature are formidable.[1] The Agricultural Prices Commission, for instance, have not done an exercise of this nature thus far and the rationale behind the prices announced by them is never made clear. Let us hope that the Planning Commission will insist on having a proper exercise done on the matter.

A buffer stock policy is also an essential ingredient of a comprehensive agricultural prices policy. But a number of issues relating to the operation of buffer stocks, such as scheduling of draw-downs and build-

[1] Interested readers may consult my 'Growth With Stability: A framework for Agricultural Planning', *Economic and Political Weekly*, Special Number, July 1968.

ups of stocks, food imports, fixing of annual levels of prices for different individual crops, etc., are intimately linked up with the evolution of a structure of relative prices. A piecemeal and *ad hoc* approach to the matter will not give a desired structure of relative prices. The whole exercise has to be done in a single, integrated framework. Given that such an exercise is done, we can then derive an appropriate composition for the buffer stock.

BUFFER STOCKS AND PROSPECTS FOR PRICE STABILITY

The Fourth Plan provides 'safeguards against the fluctuations of agricultural production'. The specific policy instrument recommended for this purpose is the operation of a sizeable buffer stock of foodgrains. This is expected to ensure that (i) consumer prices are stabilized; and (ii) 'the producers get reasonable prices and continue to have adequate incentive for increasing production'. To dramatize the importance of the buffer stock, Professor Gadgil has called it 'investment in stability'. On the question of size, the Planning Commission state that 'the setting up of a buffer stock of five million tonnes of foodgrains *might be deemed reasonably adequate*'. It is further stated that a buffer stock of this magnitude '*would suffice to meet to a significant extent all except very abnormal fluctuations*' such as those which characterized 1965-66 and 1966-67' (italics added).

The degree of protection sought by the Commission and the measure of probability with which prices are to be permitted to move *within some chosen range* are not indicated in the Plan. In the absence of clear information on those issues, it is impossible for an outsider to judge the adequacy of the size of the proposed buffer stock. But certain questions have to be confronted: what if agriculture including foodgrains, fails to grow at a trend rate of 5 per cent? Will you still build a buffer stock of five million tonnes? Even if a buffer stock of this size is built up, will you be able to ensure stable consumer prices outside of big urban centres? Would you forgo the objective of stopping PL 480 imports at the end of the next two years? Or, would you rather impose more rigorous methods of procurement? If the trend rates of growth in foodgrain production are much lower than postulated, would you resort to strict rationing and still attempt to go through the industrial programmes as envisaged in the Plan? Or, would you rather cut down the size of the Plan in the other sectors? All these questions are inter-related and the answers to these questions are not available in the

Fourth Plan. But we badly need alternatives ready for less optimistic forecasts of agricultural performance. We must also have alternative policy frames to go with each of these alternatives. Professor Gadgil had exhorted the planners in the direction of this need in 1966. Now that he is leader of the Planning Commission, we should expect the Commission to present these alternatives.

SELF-RELIANT GROWTH

The need for a strategy of self-reliance in the Fourth Plan has been seen to arise from the following two facts of the economic situations:

(1) Excessive dependence on aid in the past has laid on us a large burden of foreign debt: the heavy costs of its servicing and repayment are responsible for many difficult problems.

(2) Excessive reliance on foreign aid introduces uncertainties in planning and our aim is to provide safeguards against these uncertainties.

The Planning Commission seem to think that (a) if exports grow at a rate of 7 per cent per annum, (b) if foodgrains growth of about 5 per cent per year is backed with a buffer stock of five million tonnes, and (c) if net aid is reduced to about half its present level by the end of the Fourth Plan, then we shall be able to manage our international payments problems as well as safeguarding against uncertainties which have been threatening the continuity of even a moderate rate of growth.

Choice of a Time Horizon for Self-reliance

If a government incurs less foreign obligations today, its costs of debt servicing and repayment will be less in future. It is not equally clear, however, that its repayment capacity can stay as good if it chooses to contract very much less of foreign debt. By contracting for more foreign aid, a country not only increases its debt obligations but also increases its growth capacity and capacity for repayment in the future. There is thus a clear trade-off between self-reliance and growth. The essential decision problem is one of the choice of a time horizon for self-reliance. Otherwise, it is difficult to attach any operational meaning to self-reliance as a policy goal. If India so chooses for instance, she can stop incurring any further foreign debt obligations today and have the satisfaction of self-reliance. But this she could only do at the cost of other more pressing socio-political objectives.

A strictly self-reliant programme of growth would be one which is consistent with the assumed rate of growth of exports (i.e., 7 per cent per year) and in which any fluctuations in exports and shortfalls in import-substitution activities would be amenable to management within the available foreign exchange reserves plus our drawing rights with the International Monetary Fund. The Planning Commission have not sought this early self-reliance because it would have entailed a tight brake on our future growth as well as on our capacity for repayment of outstanding foreign obligations.

In the Fourth Plan the choice of a time horizon for self-reliance has been made: it is envisaged that net foreign aid will be eliminated by the year 1978-79. However, it is not clear how this ten-year horizon for self-reliance has been chosen. One does not know whether or not the Planning Commission considered other possible choices of time horizon that could have been made. One cannot say, for instance, that the planned growth rate of the economy during the Fourth and Fifth Plans (5·5 per cent and 6 per cent per annum respectively) and self-reliance in 1978-79 is any better or worse than the alternative of, say, 7·5 per cent growth but self-reliance in 1985 or, say, only 4·5 per cent growth and self-reliance in 1975.

One suspects that the Planning Commission have started their story of self-reliance from the wrong end. They appear to reason that, given agricultural growth at 5 per cent and export growth at 7 per cent a year and a cut in net aid to about half its current level in a period of five years, then you will achieve self-reliance at the end of the tenth year from now. A more natural way of going about the self-reliance problem would be to choose a rate and tempo of growth for the economy which might be deemed desirable on socio-political grounds. This growth will have its bundle of resource requirements, some of which might be foreign. Assuming the different levels and time distributions of these foreign resource requirements, one can work out the trade-offs between growth and early or late self-reliance; and also the trade-offs between consumption growth and the time-span for self-reliance, as well as the choice of investment pattern. The choice of an approach towards self-reliance based on such analysis could give us clear ideas of the comparative cost of relatively early and late self-reliance in terms of the social and political objectives of the nation. It would also give us an idea of the economic costs of buying greater freedom of action in internal and external affairs. Seen in this way, self-reliance (foreign aid) is better regarded as a constraint on the growth process rather than as an objective by itself.

ABSENCE OF A POLICY FRAME FOR SELF-RELIANCE

To think that, by itself, a reduction in net aid to about half its current level by the end of the Fourth Plan is going to reduce the impact on planning of uncertainties arising in the foreign sector is curious economic logic. Uncertainties in the foreign sector are caused by (i) fluctuations in export performance around the assumed trend rate, (ii) shortfalls in planned production of import substitutes, and (iii) falsification of expectations in regard to foreign aid. It may be true that by pitching your expectations of foreign aid at a modest level you may be increasing the probability of getting it. However, since the assumed level of aid is smaller, any shortfall may have proportionately large effects on the economy. The question which the Planning Commission will have to answer therefore is – how will the foreign sector of the economy be managed against these uncertainties?

Diversification of exports does provide a part of the answer. Exports of non-traditional items, however, will need to be backed up with adequate credit arrangement for their foreign buyers. Attainment of price competitiveness alone is not going to be enough since our competitors in developed countries can underbid us by throwing in an element of aid and easy credit terms. Another hint about the approach to the management of uncertainties in the foreign sector in the Fourth Plan concerns the control of trade in imported commodities. The Plan proposes that the 'import and distribution of the more important imported commodities with demand from many sources will be appropriately entrusted to relevant public agencies'. But this is only a hint. Does it mean that these public agencies would operate a buffer stock of important imported commodities? The operation of a buffer stock like this, provided these commodities are sold to the highest bidders after pre-empting the minimal requirements for strict priority sectors, could not only appropriate very sizeable illicit gains that have been accruing to private parties under the old system of import regulation, but also provide a safeguard against uncertainties. Such centralized distribution would also lead to rationalization and economies in inventory holdings.

A still better method of meeting uncertainties in the foreign sector, of course, would be to add to our foreign exchange reserves. Reserves of imported commodities would have the disadvantage of carrying costs and rigid specificities in use; whereas the foreign exchange reserves are the most malleable commodity and they can also earn a return. If the Fourth Plan is by and large a consistent plan, but does have some fat in its import requirement, and if our aid-getters can produce the expected quantum of aid and our import substitution programme makes the progress expected of it, we should lose no opportunity of adding to our reserves whenever times are good for our exports and for getting more aid. It is true that tying up of a precious resource such as foreign exchange in an unproductive fashion involves a loss in social welfare. However, the loss in social welfare that results from *ad hoc* cuts in Plan programmes which cannot be avoided when foreign exchange reserves are inadequate, is likely to be very much larger.

INVESTMENT AND OUTPUT GROWTH
IN THE FOURTH PLAN

The incremental capital output ratio (ICOR) for the Fourth Plan is given as 2·0, compared with an overall ratio of 2·4 for the first three Plan periods. The Planning Commission are of the view that this 'relatively favourable capital to output relationship during the Fourth Plan reflects (a) the possibility of securing relatively large increases in agricultural output based mainly on high-yielding varieties of seeds and the expansion of fertilizer use; (b) the existence of considerable idle capacity over a wide segment of manufacturing industries; and (c) the sizeable pipelines of investments on projects initiated during the last four to five years which are expected to bear fruit in the near future' [Fourth Plan, p. 41].

Each of these factors, which are supposed to bring about a favourable ICOR in the Fourth Plan, needs to be carefully examined. It is extremely unlikely that the volume of unfructified pipeline investment existing in 1969 is any longer than what was available at the beginning of the Third Plan. Aside from differences in the composition of investment in the two periods, the last three years of the Second Plan had witnessed a considerable step-up in the rate of investment; whereas in the three years preceding the Fourth Plan the absolute volume of investment in real terms had gone down. The case for a large reduction in the ICOR, therefore, will have to be based on the other two factors. For a proper appreciation of the extent of output growth that has been considered capable of being squeezed out of new seeds and fertilizers and existing idle capacity, a comparison between the ICOR of 2·0 in the Fourth Plan and the overall capital output ratio of 2·4 in the first three Plan periods is not meaningful. From Plan to Plan, the aggregate ICOR has been exhibiting an upward trend; therefore, difficulties that beset such interperiod comparisons of aggregate capital output ratio notwithstanding, one should instead compare the ICOR of 2·0 envisaged for the Fourth Plan with the estimate of ICOR for the Third Plan based on trend values of output. Excluding the disastrous year, 1965-66, from the Third Plan calculations, this estimate of ICOR for the Third Plan period (up to 1964-65) works out to 2·86. The point in all this is *not* that one should attach much significance to such *ex post* aggregative ratios but to make sure that they do not mislead. A better picture of output growth expected in the Fourth Plan is obtained if one makes a sector-by-sector comparison of ICORs between the Third (up to 1964-65) and the Fourth Plan. Some rough calculations of this type, following the method indicated in footnote 1 on p. 41 of the Fourth Plan document, are presented in Table One.[1]

In computing the numbers given in Table One, we had to contend with the following difficulties:

(1) The sectoral breakdowns presented here were not available in the first Three Plans. We had to make a number of assumptions before we could arrive at the estimates presented in Table One.

(2) Although the Plan Draft does give the sectoral breakdowns, our task was made difficult by the omission from the Draft Plan of figures for NDP and private investment for the year 1968-69. Only 1967-68 and 1973-74 figures by sectors are available in the Fourth Plan and one does not know what values have been assumed for 1968-69, a year which served as the base for Fourth Plan calculations.

Notice that in line four of Table One, the aggregate ICOR 2·23 for the Third Plan is based on actual NDP in 1964-65 which was considerably above its trend value and 2·23 may thus be a low estimate. The corresponding value of this ratio for the Fourth Plan works out to 2·20 or 2·27, depending upon how 1968-69 NDP estimates are worked out. It appears that the Commission's estimate of 2·0 for the ICOR in the Fourth Plan is exclusive of inventory investment. The validity of this exclusion is doubtful but if we exclude inventories, we get estimates of ICOR which are 1·98 and 2·03 on alternative assumption in regard to the base year figures.

The ICOR for the agricultural sector in the Fourth Plan works out to around 1·7 and this magnitude is much smaller than the corresponding figure of 2·3 achieved during the first four years of the Third Plan. In

---

[1] Estimates given in this table are due to my colleague, S. D. Tendulkar.

Table One

Sectoral and Aggregate Net Incremental Capital-Output Ratios with One Year Time Lag in 1967-68 Prices

(1)	I Plan (2)	II Plan (3)	III Plan (4)	IV Plan Assumption (a) (5)	IV Plan Assumption (b) (6)
1. Agriculture and Allied Sectors	1·06	2·58	2·30	1·68	1·76
2. Mining, Manufacturing and Construction	1·50	3·83	3·00	4·29	4·25
3. Transport and Communications	5·76	5·25	5·90	6·65	6·81
4. Aggregate (based on Actual NDP)	1·52	2·69	2·23	2·20	2·27
5. Aggregate (based on Exponential trend of NDP)	1·68	2·58	2·86	—	—

NOTES: (1) Definitions of Investment and Output increments are as follows:

	Investment	Output
I Plan	1951-52 to 1955-56	1956-57 over 1951-52
II Plan	1956-57 to 1960-61	1961-62 over 1956-57
III Plan	1960-61 to 1963-64	1964-65 over 1960-61
IV Plan	1969-70 to 1973-74	1974-75 over 1969-70

(2) Details of Assumptions regarding the IV Plan (page references pertain to the Draft Fourth Plan):

(i) Assumptions for getting the sectoral and aggregate NDP for 1969-70:

Assumption (a): 3·00 per cent growth rate of NDP between 1967-68 and 1968-69 (p. 5) and the implied Plan growth rate of 5·8 per cent between 1968-69 and 1969-70.

Assumption (b): 5·5 per cent Plan growth rate (p. 29) between 1968-69 and 1969-70 and implied 4·4 per cent between 1967-68 and 1968-69.

(ii) Sectoral composition of NDP for 1968-69 is assumed to be the same as in 1967-68 for 'Agriculture and Allied Sectors' and 'Mining, Manufacturing and Construction'. Then the implied Plan growth rates for these sectors based on Table Three in Chapter Two (p. 36) are used to get the sectoral outputs in 1969-70. Since no separate estimate for output of 'Transport and Communications' is given on p. 36, this sector is assumed to have the same share in 1969-70 as in 1967-68 (given on p. 57).

(iii) Total NDP and output for 'Agriculture and Allied Sectors', and 'Mining, Manufacturing and Construction', have been assumed to grow at the Fifth Plan growth rate (implied in Table Three, p. 36) between 1973-74 and 1974-75. Output for 'Transport and Communications' for 1974-75 is obtained on the assumption that this sector occupies the same share in 1974-75 as in 1973-74 (given on p. 56).

(3) Exponential trend equation for NDP is given by

$$\log_e (NDP)_t = 9\cdot0947 + 0\cdot0367t; \; R^2 = 0\cdot9831$$
(Period covered: 1950-51 to 1964-65)

the foregoing comparison one also has to remember that the year 1964-65 was a year of bumper harvest. Because of this fact the estimated ICOR of 2·30 for agriculture in the Third Plan may have already been quite favourable. For the same two periods, the ICOR for the 'mining, manufacturing and constructions' sector works out to about 4·30 (in the Fourth Plan) and 3·00 (in the Third Plan) respectively. The ICOR in 'transport and communications', a sector which is going to absorb 18·6 per cent of total investment in the Fourth Plan, is seen to go up to around 6·75 in the Fourth Plan compared to its corresponding value of 5·90 in the Third Plan. Assuming that there will be no large shifts in the composition of investment within the latter two sectors, they appear to become a lot more capital intensive in the Fourth Plan than they were in the first four years of the Third. Excess capacity in the manufacturing sector may be a physical fact of life in 1969-70, but it certainly is not implied in the ICORs worked out for the Fourth Plan. There seems to be a big cushion of fat in the Fourth Plan figures relating to the manufacturing sector.

This search points up one very important fact. It is that the favourable, aggregative ICOR envisaged in the Fourth Plan is, by and large, a consequence of assuming a very low ICOR for agriculture. This ratio is assumed to fall from 2·3 in the Third Plan to around 1·7 in the Fourth Plan. All the talk about pipeline-investment and idle capacity does not seem to account for anything with regard to the fall in the aggregate ICOR; almost the entire job is to be done by the agricultural sector. If the postulated increases in agricultural output do not materialize, the most important justification for a favourable incremental capital output ratio during the Fourth Plan would disappear.

PLAN SIZE AND NEED FOR ECONOMIC DISCIPLINE

Guided by the maxim of Self-reliant Growth with Stability, the Commission have sought to limit the extent of foreign aid and the resort to inflationary financing. The impact of this maxim on the proposed size of the Fourth Plan is that 'the outlays are modest'. It is, however, hoped by the Commission that 'even with these outlays the tempo of economic activity will be stepped up significantly in the initial years of the Plan' and 'if the performance is better, the Plan outlays in the later years could be larger than provided for now'. This prospect is seen to 'depend essentially on the extent of internal effort made in saving and investment and on the operational efficiency and economic discipline displayed by official and non-official agencies and establishments'. A point to be made is that the need for maximum operational efficiency and strict economic discipline is not only there for increasing the Plan size in later years but also for realizing the targets already laid down in the Fourth Plan.

Content of Economic and Political Discipline

Except in the matter of subsidization of exports, one sees that an attempt is being made to stop the distribution of public largesse to the not-so-poor. Food and fertilizer subsidies are being discontinued. Irrigation and power rates are being revised so that an adequate return on capital invested in these sectors is earned. Industrial and commercial undertakings in the public sector are to earn a rate of return of 15 per cent on capital employed. The need for taxation of agricultural incomes and property and for widening the base for direct taxation in general has been stressed. Increases in commodity taxation are envisaged (i) to restrain conspicuous consumption by the affluent sections of the society, (ii) to generate exportable surpluses, and (iii) to bring about a desirable allocation of productive resources. All this will do good.

However, we have two specific suggestions to make in this area. The Commission should look into the rationalization of tax structure by having the legal and economic aspects of the distinction between individuals and undivided Hindu families carefully examined. It should see if this distinction could be dropped, and also see if the time has not come for integrating the separate income tax returns of husband and wife into one.

Secondly, the Commission are silent on the question of the need for rationalizing the *ad hoc* system of export subsidies that is operative at present. The present system is not designed to ensure that export subsidization effort is focused in the direction of competitiveness in consonance with the dynamics of our comparative cost advantage. In consequence, we are not sure whether or not our efforts in promoting exports of different sectors are producing a desirable allocation of national resources.

A number of constitutional hurdles which either stand in the way of raising more resources or inhibit an efficient administration and allocation of Central funds have been talked about *ad infinitum*. The constitutional framework, in a very fundamental sense, is an instrument for the betterment of the people. If some provisions of this framework become a hindrance to development in the very early phase of its life, the only sensible thing to do is to change and amend these provisions. One wonders if, on this issue, the Commission have played their role in an adequate measure. They must impress upon the political leadership the social, economic, technical as well as the constitutional compulsions of the development problem of India. There is room for raising far more resources and we must raise them. Pressing for more development effort in the cause of faster growth and pulling up of the poor may buy a good deal of protection for our democratic institutions.

The recognition of the need for more elaborate annual planning to achieve better integration between the progress of the Five-Year Plan and budgetary policies of the Finance Ministry is a welcome feature of the new Plan. The data requirements of this task, however, are going to be large and exacting. But the degree of flexibility in steering the economy towards Plan targets that this approach may achieve would be worth the effort spent in designing and operating a live economic and Plan intelligence system.

REGULATION AND CONTROL OF THE ECONOMIC SYSTEM

An overall regulatory framework for the control of the economy – the absence of which in the three earlier Plans was considered by Professor Gadgil in 1966 as the major cause of our failures in planning – is outlined in the Plan Draft. This framework of controls is designed to ensure that (i) 'all strategic economic decisions are made by agencies informed with a social purpose', (ii) a wide 'dispersal of enterprise' and reduction in 'concentration of economic power' are achieved, and (iii) 'decentralized decision making', which is not only essential for improving operational efficiency of the economy but is also 'a value in itself', is encouraged.

Regulation of Agricultural Production and the Rural Economy

The Commission hold the view that 'in the field of agricultural production the ceiling legislation should prevent increase in concentration' (Draft Fourth Plan, p. 26). It is hoped that 'in the rural sector the extension of co-operative activity could lead to the desired combination of social purpose and decentralized decision making' (p. 25). For achieving a wide dispersal of enterprise and economic opportunities reliance has been placed on local planning through panchayati raj institutions and spread of the co-operative movement. Let us note that the present political situation in most of the States is not likely to be conducive to success in ceiling legislation. Reasonable success in injecting strength in co-operatives and panchayats would take time. As for local planning, the Commission do not seem to be clear about the operational content of it.

Control of Finance: Credit and Trade

Attaining the commanding heights of the economy via continuous expansion of productive activity in the public sector and social owner-ship of the means of production was one of the objectives of Indian socialism in the earlier Plans. Professor Gadgil seemed to be lending strong support to this objective in 1966. Now the Plan Draft proposes to regulate the economy mostly through control of credit, long-term finance, trade in foodgrains and other articles of mass consumption, and through the introduction of state trading in important imported commodities:

> In modern industry the important general allocatory controls that exist today relate to the licensing of imports and to long-term finance through public financial institutions. Effective social control of banking should lead to major decisions being informed with social purpose over the whole sphere of organized institutional credit. Outside of credit and productive activity, the major sphere is trading and storage. The Plan makes substantial provision for increasing storage capacity in the hands of public agencies. In trade the main sensitive areas are those of the allocation of scarce imported commodities, the wholesale trade in agricultural com-modities, especially foodgrains, and the distributive system in re-lation to essential goods of mass consumption. It is proposed to establish substantial control of public agencies over these sensitive areas during the Plan period. Import and distribution of the more important commodities with demand from many sources will be appropriately entrusted to relevant public agencies. The Food Corporation of India will manage the buffer stock of foodgrains, have an important share in procurement operations and will under-take inter-State movements of foodgrains. The fair price shops system will continue to be connected with food distribution. It is expected that planned growth of the co-operative distributive system linked effectively with the co-operative marketing system will take a larger share not only in distribution of foodgrains but also in distribution of other essential commodities and will reduce the margin between the prices obtained by producers and those

paid by consumers, specially for agricultural commodities (Draft Fourth Plan, pp. 25-26).

Social control over banking has been in operation for only a short time – since January 1969. It is too early to judge the results achieved thus far. A discussion of the lacunae in the policy frame which has been proposed to support the structure of social controls over wholesale trade in foodgrains has been given in the section on buffer stocks. Entrusting of imports and distribution of important imported commodities to relevant public agencies is not enough by itself; a detailed mechanism of operation is needed. The Commission, however, have given no indication of a policy frame for operating the proposed centralized control of imports.

In view of the meagre degree of success in the operation of public sector enterprises during the past fifteen years, one is unable to share the optimism of the Commission in the matter of the extensive controls that have been proposed. Management of big but compact public sector enterprises would seem to be a far easier task than socialised procurement and trade in a large number of imported and home-produced commodities over the length and breadth of the sub-continent. A bureaucracy which failed to do the former task efficiently does not inspire optimism for success in the latter.

Control of Large-Scale Industry

Modern large-scale industry in the earlier Plans has been subject to extensive investment licensing and capital issues controls. The defects in the operation of these controls have been well documented. For reduction of concentration of economic power, the Plan now looks in an entirely different direction. It looks towards the monopolies legislation, social control of banks and appropriate fiscal policy. In the fiscal policy chapter of the Plan, however, one looks in vain for an integrated structure of fiscal action which might combat inequalities and reduce concentration of economic power. For control over the location of industry the Fourth Plan recommends (a) the provision of positive assistance and incentives for dispersal of industry and (b) the imposition of disincentives in large cities and metropolitan areas.

In view of the present 'much greater availability within the country of plant, machinery and other equipment needed to establish new industrial enterprises', the Commission favour a relaxation of control over industrial investment. However, the way in which the Planning

Commission have argued their case is intriguing. Witness, for instance, the following:

> On assumption, therefore, *that* the monopolies legislation and social controls of banking will be operative in desired directions, *that* developments in crucial industrial fields will be fully planned and *that* trading in sensitive areas will be in the hands of public agencies, a revision of the present regime of control appears desirable and is proposed. (p. 26, italics added).

That this proposal is highly conditional is obvious.

Operation of the Public Sector

In the context of the need for economic discipline, the Commission have drawn special attention to the operation of the public sector which has belied the original expectation of yielding 'substantial resources for its continued development'. In view of this failure and the general resource constraints, 'only limited increase in public sector industrial activity has been proposed in the Plan'. This represents a marked change in strategy of Indian Planning. This de-emphasis of the public sector appears to have been justified – first because of its inability to generate resources for its continued growth; and second, because the removal of basic deficiencies in the economic structure is seen to have already been achieved.

In the matter of the public sector's inability to generate resources for its continued growth, the Commission have recommended action along two lines. First is 'in the direction of much greater co-ordination and integration' of the activities of the various public sector units by 'creating appropriate machinery for effective co-ordination'; and, secondly, they propose that 'detailed decision making in the individual units should be effectively decentralized'.

These are good suggestions, but they would not go far enough in getting the job done. A major need at present is to develop technical expertise in the field of economic and industrial management. General purpose administrators are ill-suited for managing complex industrial enterprises in the public sector. They must be replaced by production and management experts. Incentives and promotions for public sector managers should be given in relation to their performance on given jobs rather than on the basis of seniority. No tenure positions need be offered and inefficient managers could be ruthlessly eliminated. This would impart a measure of competitiveness in public sector management. Another method of introducing an element of competitiveness in public sector enterprises would be through *not* meeting their requirements of maintenance imports. For some proportion of these import requirements they may be made to compete with other users or made to pay proportionately higher prices.

A most important factor militating against operational efficiency in the public sector, however, has been confusion of objectives. A government which aims at accumulation of capital in its hands, should get rid of the overhang of 'public utility' ideas of public sector operation and pricing practised in *laissez-faire* economies. It is about time we shook off this confusion of thought in regard to public sector enterprises and insisted on their meeting profitability criteria consistent with the needs of efficient operation and future growth.

Nevertheless, the view that public enterprises are not here for making profits still persists. The Commission have clearly seen the necessity of an adequate rate of return being earned by commercial and industrial undertakings in the public sector; however, they have yet to convince the politicians of this necessity. The point to make sure is that such returns are *not* earned merely on the basis of their exercise of monopolistic power and by adding this margin in their full-cost pricing policies. Efforts should be made to see that they are competitive as well as efficient in their operations.

THE POOR AND THE WEAK

An outstanding feature of the Fourth Plan is that it places a very conspicuous and oft-repeated emphasis on 'the common man, the weaker sections and the less privileged'. It is laid down by the Commission 'that planning *should* result in greater equality in income and wealth' and 'that benefits of development *should* accrue more and more to the relatively less privileged classes of society'. For achieving greater equality in incomes and levels of living and ameliorating the economic conditions of the poor, the weak and the less privileged, three distinct types of policies are available to a Government:

(1) It can adopt redistribution through fiscal, pricing and other policies.

(2) It can force the pace of growth in the economy and in the process, along with other sections of the society, pull up the poor and the weak.

(3) It can take deliberate and specific policy measures to improve the productivity of the weaker units and regions and widen opportunities

of education, productive work and employment for the common man and the less privileged sections.

Growth Versus Redistribution

The view expressed in the Fourth Plan is that in a poor country like India no significant results can be achieved through redistributive policies since 'whatever surpluses can be mobilized from the higher incomes of the richer classes are needed for investment in the economy to lay the basis for larger consumption in the future'. The poor and the weak, therefore, have to be helped through faster growth of the economy and other specific policy measures. The conflict between growth and redistribution has been in the forefront of discussions of Indian planning. The view taken in the Fourth Plan is a somewhat sharper echo of the views in the earlier Plans. Let us, however, see what the growth process in India has done to the levels of living of the poor in the past.

The Poor Over Time

In Table Two, the average *per capita* private consumption of different fractile groups in 1957-58 and 1960-61 are presented. Notice that after ten years of planning, the overall average *per capita* private consumption in 1960-61 was Rs. 271 per year; for the poorest 5 per cent, however, it was only Rs. 65 and the richest 5 per cent had an average consumption of Rs. 818. On some yardsticks, even the rich of India (i.e. the top 5 per cent of the population) will look poor. Nonetheless, our concern here is with the real poor, the weak and the less privileged; and for separating them from the relatively rich, we need a criterion. One such criterion was provided by a working group[1] in July 1962. They had recommended a standard of private consumption expenditure of Rs. 240 *per capita* per year as a bare minimum. Looking at Table Two, it is clear that right through 1967-68 almost half, or more, of the population of India was living in abject poverty. On the basis of rough interpolations in Table Two, a lower bound on the number of people below the minimum level of living during the past ten years, and similar projections for the future based on the long-term perspective in the Draft Fourth Plan, have been worked out. These numbers are given in Table Three.

[1] This group was comprised of Professor D. R. Gadgil, Dr B. N. Ganguli, Dr P. S. Lokanathan, Shri M. R. Masani, Shri Asoka Mehta, Shri Shriman Narayan, Shri Pitambar Pant, Dr V. K. R. V. Rao, and Shri Anna Saheb Sahasrabuddhe. Included in this list are five persons who, at one time or the other, have served on the Planning Commission.

Table Two

Average *per capita* Consumption by Fractile Groups

Fractile group	Average *per capita* consumption at 1960-61 prices in rupees						
	1957-58	1960-61	1967-68	1973-74	1973-74	1980-81	1980-81
(1)	(2)	(3)	(4)	(5)	(6)	(7)	(8)
0-5	61	65	77	88	93	108	130
5-10	87	93	108	122	129	151	175
10-20	112	119	136	154	161	191	213★
20-30	139	149	167	190	196	234★	257
30-40	166	177	197	224★	230★	277	296
40-50	196	209★	229★	260	264	322	337
50-60	227★	243	265	300	304	372	384
60-70	267	285	307	349	350	431	436
70-80	319	341	363	412	412	510	504
80-90	400	427	449	509	501	630	606
90-95	512	546	565	641	624	793	738
95-100	767	818	822	932	893	1153	1023
All groups	254	271	290	329	329	407	407
			(494)†	(559)†		(692)†	
Mid-year population (millions)	411	436	514	596	596	690	690
Concentration index	0·335	0·335	0·311	0·311	0·300	0·311	0·275

† Average *per capita* private consumption in 1967-68 prices.

Table Three

Percentage of Population Below a Minimum Level of Living

Year	per cent	Population (in millions)
1957-58	58	238
1960-61	54	235
1967-68	48	247
1973-74	39	232
	(38)	(226)
1980-81	27	186
	(21)	(145)

Allowing for errors of NSS estimates which have provided the basis for these calculations, it is fair to conclude that between 1957-58 and 1967-1968 the number of people below a normative poverty line has stayed pretty nearly constant around 240 million. The proportion of population in this category during the same period, however, has fallen from 58 per cent to 48 per cent. This is largely a consequence of the increase in overall *per capita* consumption from Rs. 254 in 1957-58 to Rs. 290 in 1967-68; the slight fall in the concentration index (Lorenz ratio), from 0·335 in 1957-58 to 0·311 in 1967-68 contributed very little. The *per capita* private consumption during this period grew at a rate of 1·33 per cent per year; *per capita* net national product at 1·62 per cent and population at 2·28 per cent per year.

Assuming that no new redistributive measures will be effective during the Fourth Plan period and in later years up to 1980-81, the projected levels of consumption (which are consistent with the rates of income growth of the long-term perspective in the Draft Fourth Plan) in 1973-74 and 1980-81 will look as in columns 5 and 7 of Table Two. At least 39 per cent of the population in 1973-74 and 27 per cent in 1980-81 will be below the minimum level of living; the number of people in this category will still be 232 million and 186 million respectively. These are very large numbers. Even if all goes well and in accordance with Plans, thirty years of national planning will not have pulled up at least 186 million people out of abject poverty.

There is a good deal of talk in the Plan document about effective implementation of ceiling legislation on agricultural land and other specific policy measures to improve the productivity of weaker units and regions. Let us, for the time being, assume that these measures meet with a good measure of success in reducing inequalities in consumption levels. Let us say that these policy measures will reduce the concentration index from 0·311 in 1967-68 to 0·300 in 1973-74 and to 0·275 in 1980-81. This reduction in inequality may not occur, but let us note that this is not too much to expect. A lognormal distribution appears to give an adequate representation of the household expenditure distribution in 1967-68 (and also in 1960-61 as well as in 1957-58). Assuming that lognormality of population distribution by *per capita* expenditure levels will hold in 1973-74 as well as in 1980-81 and that the overall average *per capita* consumption levels respectively of Rs. 329 and Rs. 407 (in 1960-61 prices) will materialize in these years, the levels of living by fractile groups will look as in columns 6 and 8 of Table Two. The impact of these reductions in the concentration index on the percentage as well as on the numbers of people below the poverty line in 1973-74 and 1980-81 are recorded in Table Three (in parenthesis). We shall still have 145 million (in comparison with 186 million when no change in concentration is assumed) people below the bare minimum level of living in 1980-81. These, then, are the prospects for the poor, the weak and the less privileged of independent India after thirty years of planning. An increase of approximately 13 per cent in average *per capita* consumption by 1973-74, over its 1967-68 level, does not appear to reduce significantly the number of people below the bare minimum. If no reduction in the concentration index takes place during this period, there will be 232 million of miserably poor people at the end of the Fourth Plan; with a mild fall in inequality this number would drop to 226 million.

Specific Programmes and Policies for the Small Man and Weaker Units

The Commission are aware that the consumption standards of the poor are not going to improve 'unless special efforts are made during this period (next ten years) to alter the existing pattern of distribution of income'. The possibility of progress in the desired direction during the Fourth Plan depends on the success of a number of programmes proposed in the Plan. Included in this list of programmes are, for example, the special package schemes for small farmers (package schemes for big farmers have already been there), programmes of animal husbandry to support the economy of small farmers and landless labourers, administration of forestry schemes to benefit contiguous rural areas and forest labourers and dwellers, long-term programmes of rehabilitation and development on a viable basis of individual rural industries, measures for dispersal of industry and for the protection of and continuous technological progress in small scale industries, a pilot project to test the possibility of making a standing offer of employment to local labour in certain areas, pilot experiments in about twenty selected districts for setting up of Small Farmers' Development Agency in each one of them and so on. The physical outlines and preliminary feasibility studies of these programmes and schemes are nowhere in sight. The extent of financial provisions for these schemes in the Plan is also not clear. All this, then, is in the realm of good intentions.

The broad approach suggested in the Plan for ameliorating the income distribution problem of the poor and the weak is one of area and activity development. The Commission have indicated that they are equipping themselves 'to be in a position to assist the States in the preparation and evaluation of individual projects and programmes and also in dealing with the overall problems of regional and district planning'. All of this effort in the direction of decentralization of planning may lead to good results, but the effort has yet to start.

It is no doubt good to have good intentions, but in the examples cited above one also gets an indication of wishful thinking on the part of the Commission. The *seriatim* approach, in which the poor will get prior attention not only from the government but also from credit co-operatives (controlled by the big) and land development banks, will have no in-built compulsion for its adoption. Now that a formula has been adopted for the distribution of Central assistance to the States, and 20 per cent of the total quantum of Central assistance is to go to the poor States and special problem areas, will it not be better if, in the siting of Central projects, efficiency considerations dominate? Endless mixing up of equity and efficiency will make for a falling between the two stools. If the Commission are not satisfied with the pace at which poorer States and backward sections would improve their economic conditions at present levels of Central assistance, then they should increase the level of Central assistance itself or provide incentives to the States for raising more resources for these programmes.

Fourth Plan's Progress towards Economic Democracy

The relevant information on the public sector outlays on education, health and social welfare – the Third Plan actuals and the Fourth Plan proposals are given in Table Four. These are the outlays which benefit the poor more than the rich. This should reflect the real degree of concern that the Commission have for the establishment of economic democracy. Excluding investments in housing and urban development which have mostly benefited the rich, the *per capita* investment in the cause of economic democracy during the Fourth Plan period works out to Rs. 23·2. Recalling all the fond names by which the Fourth Plan has called the poor to memory, each one of them may get around Rs. 5 worth of additional services per year directed towards their economic and social improvement or to reduction of their numbers. In the Fourth Plan, there is no step-up in *per capita* outlays in this sector as compared with the Third Plan.[1] In the case of education, *per capita* outlay (in

[1] The absolute amounts spent on these services have, of course, been rising over time. The point that is being made here is that their rate of expansion is now being slowed down. A large share of the responsibility for this slow-down, probably, rests with the States

1960-61 prices) in the Fourth Plan (of Rs. 0·84) is less than the *per capita* outlay (of Rs. 1·13) in the Third Plan. One should not, however,

Table Four

Public Sector Outlays on Education, Health and Social Welfare

		Third Plan outlay* (1960-61 prices)	Third Plan actual ex-penditure (current prices)	Fourth Plan outlay (1968-69 prices)
(0)	(1)	(2)	(3)	(4)
		(Rs crores)		
1.	General education	418·1	463·9	681·8
2.	Technical education	141·6	124·8	119·8
3.	Scientific research	70·0	71·4	134·0
4.	Health ⎫		225·9	437·5
5.	Family planning ⎬	341·8	24·9	300·0
6.	Water supply ⎭		105·7	338·9
7.	Welfare of backward classes	113·9	99·1	134·9
8.	Social welfare	27·6	19·4	37·2
9.	Labour welfare and craftsman training	71·1	55·8	37·1
10.	Public co-operation ⎫			
11.	Local and rural works ⎭	50·3	36·9	—
12.	Total (1 to 11)	1234·4	1227·8	2220·6
13.	Housing and urban development	142·0	127·5	170·7
14.	Total (12 + 13)	1376·4	1355·3	2391·3
15.	Average population (millions)	467	467	568
	Per Capita outlay:			
16.	Excluding housing (Rs.)	26·4†	26·3‡	39·1§
17.	Including housing (Rs.)	29·5†	29·0‡	42·1§
	Per capita outlay at 1960-61 prices			
18.	Excluding housing (Rs.)	26·4	23·3¶	23·2‖
19.	Including housing (Rs.)	29·5	25·6	25·0

* This represents the total cost of physical programmes included in the Third Plan originally contemplated.

† At 1960-61 prices.

‡ At current prices.

§ At 1968-69 prices.

¶ At 1960-61 prices—deflator used is 113, i.e. the Third Plan average index of prices over 1960-61 as base.

‖ Wholesale price index deflator, 1968-69 over 1960-61 of 168·3 is used in converting Fourth Plan outlay to 1960-61 prices.

forget the change in the composition of education between the Third and the Fourth Plan. We have succeeded in producing our engineering complement of manpower: now that tens of thousands of them are unemployed, in the Fourth Plan period we will invest in more primary education, which is cheaper. The outlay on family planning in the Fourth Plan is very much larger than it was in the Third. It is apparently hoped that in the future the rich may get richer but the poor will have fewer children.

MISSED OPPORTUNITIES

In 1969 there are 245 to 250 million Indian citizens who are below a bare minimum level of living. Incidence of this abject poverty is not uniform all over the country. A very large proportion of these dismally poor people are concentrated in a few well-defined regions. The overall pace of growth in the country over the last eighteen years has not been fast enough to make an appreciable difference in their levels of living. They have begun to take an interest in the procedures of a political democracy and they have had some educational benefits; their expectations are rising every day and so also are their frustrations. Strong class feelings on economic lines are emerging. Indiscipline in public life and intense competition of a low order among political parties during the last few years have led to further complications, which are adding to the frustrations of the poor. They are becoming restive. Organized violence is on the increase. Unless an appreciable change in the levels of living of the poor is ensured, and that pretty fast too, the very fabric of Indian democracy will be in jeopardy. It is in this context that the Fourth Plan will have to be judged. Seen this way the Plan does not come to grips with the basic problem of Indian development.

In the last year of the Fourth Plan (1974), for instance, there will still be 225 to 235 million people below a bare minimum level of living. Under the maxim of *Self-reliant Growth with Stability* and constrained by a level of availability of additional financial resources which has been considered feasible, Plan outlays of a modest size are proposed. Stability of prices has been given an overriding consideration because the sharp price rises of the past few years have been held responsible for the erosion of 'resources for financing development'. It is true that galloping inflation and deep recession are inimical to growth. But to suggest that rising prices over the past few years have eroded savings is tantamount to putting the cart before the horse. The root cause of this problem of resources has not been the rising prices *per se* but the slowness of growth in the economy. The irony of it all is that the consequential paucity of public financial resources, once again, is being pressed in as the main reason for the modest size of the Fourth Plan. We are caught in a vicious circle. Still another vicious circle is implicit in the argument of the Commission which says that we cannot grow fast because financial resources are limited, and we cannot do much by way of redistributive justice or through the provision of socialised consumption for the poor because we want to grow fast in an environment of price stability. The poor get the short end of it on both counts.

A natural question to ask, therefore, is: will the large masses of the poor have the patience to wait until we develop the necessary will to break out of these vicious circles? The air is so tense with anxiety and the political situation in certain parts of the country so grim that an answer in the affirmative can hardly be ventured. The impatience of the poor with their lot is already evident. If we fail to accelerate the improvement in their opportunities and living standards, their discontent will turn out to be a potent political force capable of destroying the very foundations of the system that we have been trying to build. The political stability of the republic is in peril. The need of the hour is to speed up the rate of growth of the economy and also to modify the income generation process in favour of the poor through imaginative programmes and policies, so that they can benefit and develop a stake in the continuance of our democratic system. It is only with clarity of purpose, imagination and, above all, political courage that the difficulties inherent in our situation can be overcome. The Planning Commission have all but missed their opportunity in the Draft Fourth Plan to grasp the compulsions of Indian poverty and to focus the nation's attention on the courses open to us.

Discussion of Dr B. S. Minhas' Paper

Opening the discussion of Minhas' paper, Professor Hanson declared he would concentrate on what he knew most about: the rapidly changing socio-political conditions in which planning was taking place and the likely effect of these on the character of the planning exercise.

With the change of management, nearly two years ago, the Planning Commission had acquired a Deputy Chairman, Professor Gadgil, who had previously been one of the strongest critics of its policies and procedures. Their major vice, from his point of view, was that they had combined vague and over-generalized objectives with the 'total absence of a policy frame'.

By 'policy frame' he meant something quite different from the Waterstonian 'action programme'. He was demanding, in fact, the installation of a battery of controls far more comprehensive and co-ordinated than any previously attempted. More importantly, he insisted that this should be informed by and operated in accordance with a consistent 'philosophy' of economic development, of a specifically socialist kind. His tendency was to regard whatever was not planned and regulated by the public authorities as something that had 'got away' – and one could well imagine that the booming private enterprise economy of the Punjab was not a phenomenon that he could greet with unalloyed approval.

Now, Gadgil as Deputy Chairman had produced a plan that was not substantially different in kind from previous plans. There were, of course, changes in proportion and in emphasis, but none of philosophy or of method. Why should this be? The most obvious reason was that Gadgil was no longer a free agent; but there were also more specific reasons. Of these, three seemed to Professor Hanson to be particularly important.

The first lay in the very nature of Five-Year Plans. It was difficult to get away from the kind of document which first stated objectives in quantitative terms and then offered some general indication of the policy instruments available to secure their fulfilment. It could be dangerously premature to attempt a definition of precisely how these instruments should be used, in changing circumstances of an imperfectly predictable kind. As had been constantly emphasized by other speakers, flexibility was of the essence of the planning exercise. Therefore it seemed that Minhas was a little hard on Gadgil in demanding of him that his plan should contain a 'detailed mechanism of operation' needed for dealing with such things as 'imports and distribution of important commodities'.

Secondly, it had to be remembered that the Fourth Plan was the *fourth* plan, which took as its starting-point the end-products of the previous plans. Among these were a variety of *unplanned* results of a socio-political kind. Minhas himself emphasized the 'distribution of public largesse to the not-so-poor'. This had helped to create a distribution of economic resources and political power (the two things tended to coincide in the India of today) which was *incompatible* with the type of planning that Gadgil had advocated and which Minhas appeared to present, sometimes in successive paragraphs, as both essential and impracticable.

Thirdly, there was the immediate political situation: the loss of Congress dominance, the political chaos that had overtaken several of the States, the replacement of the old national leadership by one that drew its strength from local and regional party machines, the change in the balance of power as between New Delhi and the State capitals. All this had made the type of planning embodied in the Second and Third Plans very much more difficult, and the type formerly advocated by Gadgil completely Utopian.

These facts of political life, however, had not as yet *fully* impressed themselves on the minds of the planners, who showed a rather depressing tendency to go through the old motions. Minhas displayed acute schizophrenia. In one paragraph he deplored the 'basic attitude of the Indian people towards the government' and said that this could be overcome only 'through the exercise of disciplined and purposive political and administrative action', the need for which was 'even more essential now than at any time in the past'. He engaged, in fact, in the same kind of hortatory exercise for which he blamed the Planning Commission. Then, in the very next paragraph, he condemned his own utopianism by saying that 'the chances of success in this regard do not look good at all'. To make a demand in the strongest possible terms and then to expose it as unrealistic was – Professor Hanson wished to say without giving offence – rather characteristic of the Indian intellectual, who tended to combine perfectionism with disillusionment in a curious and fascinating amalgam. Such a combination was well illustrated by Gadgil himself.

What, then, were the prospects for Indian planning? The paper answered this question with a kind of muffled optimism qualified by political forebodings.

A discouraging feature of the Draft Fourth Plan, which it shared – as it shared its virtues – with the two previous plans, was that it based its detailed predictions and targets on over-optimistic assumptions. This was the case, for instance, with the incremental capital output ratio, which was brought down to a not very meaningful aggregate of 2·27 by dint of assuming a fall from 2·3 to 1·7 for agriculture. It was also the case with the proclaimed objective of 'building up . . . an integrated structure for establishing social and economic democracy particularly in the countryside'. About this, Minhas' critical remarks seemed to Professor Hanson quite conclusive. Indeed, one might perhaps be glad that the Commission were not likely to make much progress towards a rural democracy of the sort that it vaguely envisaged, since, given the characteristics of Indian rural society, such a democracy would almost certainly be incompatible with the raising of the level of agricultural production by the required amount. However, all this was very much the mixture as before. It had been ably exposed by Minhas and hardly called for further comment. But Professor Hanson did want to call attention to Minhas' excellent remarks on the insufficiency of self-sufficiency as an objective, which concluded with the challenging statement that 'self-reliance is better regarded as a restraint on the growth process rather than an objective by itself'.

He turned, finally, to the political forebodings. Minhas found the situation ominous (appearing to be in agreement with Selig Harrison and Neville Maxwell rather than with Myron Weiner and Morris Jones), and envisaged the possibility that planning itself might come to a sticky end.

As a *sine qua non* for salvation, Minhas emphasized an 'appreciable change in the standard of living of the poor' which he said had to take place 'pretty fast'. Was this possible? Professor Hanson did not think so. It was certainly not possible in the context of the Plan as drafted, and would probably not be possible under any alternative kind of Plan – even one that was considerably bigger, differently oriented in respect of the distribution in income and wealth, and carried out with unprecedented vigour. But Minhas' assumptions about the behaviour of the poor must not pass unquestioned. Was it likely that they would mount a revolt that would not only disrupt the Plan, but bring to an end India's twenty-year-old experiment in democracy? Professor Hanson did not know, nor did anyone else; but experience suggested that such a revolt was less likely to occur when the poor remained poor than when they were beginning to get richer and to develop new economic ambitions and wider cultural horizons. This in itself, of course, was a dangerous generalization; but he suggested that Minhas' views about the relationship between poverty and revolt were somewhat simplistic and demanded more rigorous examination than Minhas had chosen to give them.

More serious was Minhas' emphasis on the growing 'indiscipline' in public life and the 'intense competition of low order among political parties'. The big question this raised was whether India was on the edge of political chaos or in the process of making an admittedly difficult transition to a new type of 'bargaining' political culture. Again, no one knew; but for purposes of argument we had to assume the latter, since acceptance of the former would reduce all our discussions about planning to the level of sheer futility.

If such a transition was taking place, its effect on planning would be profound. Indeed, political changes, as we had seen, have already made planning very different from what it used to be. Their impact was seen in the 'downgrading' of the Commission and in the great difficulties it had experienced in securing acceptance of the Draft Plan by some of the States. There was now a new emphasis on political compromise in the planning process, at the expense of emphasis on economic rationality. If this was not to make a mockery of national planning, there was an obvious need for a more serious type of consultation than any hitherto attempted with 'interests' of all kinds, regional, functional and political. Among other things, far greater importance had to be attached to discussion at the National Development Council, which had until now been little more than an organ for giving generalized – but rarely very serious – approval to decisions that the Commission and the Government have already taken.

Professor Hanson concluded on a rather gloomy note. The fact was that (to use Myrdal's terminology) India was a 'soft' State which was becoming softer. In default of revolutionary changes, which did not appear likely, the planning process would have to adapt itself, for good or ill, to this situation. The Planning Commission had not really faced it as yet – to judge by the content of the Draft Outline. But it was something that would *have* to be faced, if planning were to become a more realistic, if less heroic exercise.

Following Professor Hanson, Mr Lipton said that, partly because the Indians were the most self-critical planners in the world, Indian planning was judged by standards very much more severe than those applied to planning in any other country in the world. For instance, what was meant by instability? Was India not politically stable, having withstood two fantastically severe droughts and two near-wars in three years, at the end of which the swing against Congress was substantially less than the swing against the British Conservative Party in the general election of 1966? If that country was not stable, almost hyperstable, Mr Lipton was at a loss to know what stability meant.

Mr Lipton then passed on to the main point: the discussion of agriculture. He agreed very warmly with Dr Minhas' memorable phrase: 'the chatter about the green revolution'. There had been far too much of this – and from economists rather than agronomists. Agronomists were extremely cautious about the limits of this sort of seed improvement. It was economists, on the whole, who had jumped over the moon in the projections of how long this was likely to continue and how much it was likely to produce. Three things had to be explained together: the persistent over-optimism of Indian agricultural planning, even relative to Indian planning in other sectors of the economy; the fact that the allocation of investible resources to Indian agriculture had been too small; and severe misallocations within agriculture such as those discussed by Dr Minhas. On the second point, Mr Lipton was unable to accept any argument that investment allocations to agriculture had not been too small. While accepting that the marginal capital output ratios listed in Minhas' paper were only indicative, the differences in the ICORs for agriculture on the one hand, and mining, manufacturing and construction on the other were so large as to cast heavy doubts on the efficiency of the proposed allocations. Of course, capital was not the only scarce factor. There were others, but agriculture tended to use less of those as well. Moreover, capital was many factors and not one; the composition of marginal capital going into agriculture was such as to generate fewer strains particularly in terms of foreign exchange and ancillary skills than the capital going into industry. On this level, whatever the doubts about calculations, something had gone very wrong in the allocation of resources to agriculture. Somehow, agriculture had got fewer resources than made sense on any sensible criteria, and the Fourth Plan did very little to correct this. The current draft was better in this respect than the 1966 version, the allocation to agriculture having risen from 21·1 per cent of public development outlay to 21·8 per cent. That was still less than in any other previous plan or draft outline, except the 1966 exercise.

All this seemed explicable to Mr Lipton in terms of the political system. There was no conspiracy afoot, but politicians were following their own interests by avoiding trouble in the urban sector. The way of

doing this was to extract the surplus, and that meant giving the fertilizers and credit to the rich farmers. This was not because of social bias
in favour of the rich, but because the rich farmers sold the surplus food
to the towns. So in order to keep all the vested interests, and particularly
the potentially revolutionary urban vested interests, more or less happy,
this was the way the system sorted itself out. The persistent over-
optimism was also explained, because if the whole system were urban
biased, it would be ignorant of real rural returns and realities. In any
case, the bias of research towards the urban sector was no political
accident. As for the under-allocation to agriculture, that was obviously
explained in terms of pressure by industrialists for infrastructural
investment to keep electric power, railway freight, and so on cheap for
private investors and industry. The misallocation within agriculture was
explained largely by the fact that resources had gone to the people producing surpluses. Yet there was now a very large body of evidence
showing that in India, down to a really small level of holding, the
smaller the holding, the larger the output per acre for that holding.
Unfortunately, the small farmer would eat it himself; he would not sell
it to the town, and therefore the politicians were not terribly interested
in the output he produced, and therefore resources were misallocated.

Mr Lipton conceded that he may have been a bit harsh about the
green revolution. There were many countries in the world where a green
revolution was reality – the Philippines, for example, in spite of recent
setbacks. The green revolution was a reality for any country which had
reliable water supply and not an absolute land famine, because the new
seeds worked in conditions of reliable water supply and water control.
On a very generous estimate, not more than 25 per cent of India's land
could possibly enjoy what could be described as reliable water control
by the end of the Fourth Plan period. On this land, not more than one
in three farmers could possibly enjoy *either* access to reasonably cheap
co-operative credit *or* resources of their own such as would enable them
to buy these new factors without paying 25-45 per cent rate of interest
to the money-lender so that the innovation was not profitable. Consequently, since it was on the irrigated land that there was a greater
preponderance of smaller farmers, and fragmentation had gone much
further, a one in twelve estimate (one in four times one in three) was an
upper estimate of the Indian farmers whom the green revolution would
reach by 1974. On top of that, in the Indian environment the new
techniques had produced dramatic effects only for wheat, but not yet
for rice.

Minhas' discussion of inequality was interesting and impressive. This approach was the most serious and interesting attempt to quantify forward what was going to happen in income distribution in India that Mr Lipton had seen, and the prospect was extremely worrying. The conclusions to be drawn from it were posed by the question: Do we really have to face this harsh alternative between either inequality and growth, or equality and no growth? If it was that harsh, then the chips were down. But he felt that there was not very much evidence that it was that harsh – certainly not in agriculture, and certainly not if the small farmer made, on the whole, more productive use of resources. Apart from the weakening of the argument for inequality on the grounds mentioned earlier, it was further weakened by the fact that, in the rural sector, one man's saving was usually not investment, but another man's dissaving. The money-lender saved so that the man living below subsistence could dissave by borrowing and hence spend more than his income. This form of gross inequality in the rural sector created dissaving as well as saving, invalidating the assumption that the saving of the rich gets turned into investment.

Mr Lipton felt that the inequality effects of the green revolution would be terribly complicated. It could not be assumed that it would necessarily make matters worse. If it made food cheaper, all net buyers of food would benefit. In particular, landless labourers would benefit because of falling food prices, and in so far as extra jobs were created they would benefit too. The small minority – at most 8 or 9 per cent of peasants – who get the seeds would benefit also, because they would obtain much more output at low cost, and hence higher profits. So the top 8 or 9 per cent, and in the rural sector perhaps the bottom 15-20 per cent (net food buyers), would benefit. But the large, middle sector of poor peasants, who had some surplus to sell the town but not much, would lose because of the falling level of food prices over time implied by a successful green revolution. If the Indian Government did get anywhere near its target of 5 per cent growth per year in grain output, then the large middle section would find prices falling, on normal elasticity assumptions, by something not very far short of 5 per cent. Prices could not be maintained indefinitely against that relative trend of supply and demand. The depression in the real incomes of the large middle section would result in a very interesting and quite complicated rural distribution situation, for which one would like to think political as well as economic provision was being made.

Mr Lipton concluded by suggesting that the 1-1½ per cent to which

Dr Minhas reduced the Planning Commission's forecast for agricultural growth was still considerably too optimistic. If he had to put his shirt on a figure, it would be 3½ per cent and he thought they would be doing extremely well to achieve that, partly because Dr Minhas' estimate of past trends were substantially biased by including the years 1952-53 and 1953-54, in each of which output grew by 10 per cent consequent on a law-and-order improvements, recovery from the effects of refugees, and perhaps better data. These observations could not really be taken as part of any long-term trend, and if they were neglected, then the pre-1964 performance of Indian agriculture did not look nearly as happy as it did on Minhas' account.

The problem of India, as far as foreign exchange was concerned, appeared, in an extraordinary way, to have some things in common with the United States. In both cases, there were very small export-income ratios, never anything like 10 per cent and usually nearer 5 per cent. In both cases, there was an inflow of external capital which was quite small (sometimes negative) relative to total capital requirements. (This was, of course, much more relevant in India, with its finance constraints on total investment.) By the standards of the less developed world, the proportion of investment financed by foreign aid was not large, the figure being about 13 per cent. What really needed explanation was the apparent difficulty in making a foreign exchange effort which was very small relative to gross national product.

The general discussion which followed focused on three main themes: the overall political and economic prospects, with a heavy emphasis on growth and redistribution issues; agriculture; and aid and trade.

The first note of foreboding was sounded very early on by Professor Reddaway. Although it was commonly assumed that a 'solution' to the Indian problem did exist, he wanted to question such an assumption. Perhaps there was no 'solution', especially in terms of averting the development of a potentially revolutionary situation. Yet one had still to pose the question: what should the Planning Commission do? To criticize the content of the plan document without offering constructive advice, as Minhas had done, seemed to him to be hypocritical. There was also the key role of population growth in generating poverty. That had to be slowed as a necessary condition for a solution to be found.

These issues were subsequently taken up by Lord Balogh. If there were no solution, then the conclusion was that certain things could not be avoided. The thorny problem of redistribution could not be brushed off by references to the Indian character – events in China had exploded that kind of myth. Viewed as a political manifesto, the Plan certainly had its uses and the Planning Commission was right to exploit that aspect of it. It was disturbing, however, to see that outlays on health and education were being cut down. Moreover there was still no reform of the educational system which, reinforced by caste, had produced anti-modernization and anti-growth attitudes.

Mr Zinkin adopted a very different position. Growth and inequality, he argued, were quite inseparable. A skilled worker in a steel plant would inevitably receive a higher income than a small peasant farmer. If there was to be growth in agriculture, most of it had to occur in the Punjab where there was assured water supply, rather than other regions which were not similarly endowed. Moreover, professional people would always get above average incomes and continuing growth depended on an increasing supply of their skills. On a related point, there was also the fact that the focus of political power had changed. In the post-independence period up to a few years ago, power had been held by upper-class intellectuals with a guilt complex. But in recent years, power had shifted to the top 10 per cent (maybe even 25-30 per cent) of rural households – that is, to the bigger farmers. This group had no passion for redistribution, just as the evidence pointed to an aversion on the part of the landless to taking their neighbours' land as distinct from the land of city absentees.

Some interesting rule-of-thumb calculations offered by Mr Waterston also cast doubt on the political feasibility of some of the Plan proposals. If the Planning Commission's optimism concerning agriculture turned out to be misplaced and the rate of growth of agricultural output stayed at about 3·5 per cent, then a rate of growth in GDP of 5 per cent would imply a growth rate of 8 to 9 per cent in the industrial sector and a savings-income ratio of about 20 per cent. Further, if the growth in exports was kept at 7 per cent, then consumption would have to be squeezed still more. The upshot was that taxes would have to rise by about 9 per cent if price stability were to be maintained, and that the incidence of the tax burden would have to fall overwhelmingly on the urban sector. This order of magnitude, Waterston suggested, was on the limit.

The employment issue, or rather its absence, was raised by Dr Papanek. The lack of discussion of the unemployment problem was compared unfavourably with plans published in other Asian countries, in Africa, and in Latin America. In political terms, the marginally employed urban worker was not only badly off, but also a focus for dis-content. Perhaps the silence on this point was an indication of despair.

Inevitably, there was some discussion of trend rates of growth. If 1947 were taken as the base year, then the trend value fell from 3·1 per cent, as calculated by Minhas, to 2·8 per cent per annum. On this showing, not only Minhas, but also Lipton was over-optimistic. Another view contested the validity of the methodology of extrapolating the future from past trends. Taking the example of Ceylon, it was pointed out that its agricultural sector had grown at between 4 to 4·5 per cent per year throughout the fifties and early sixties. Yet the four years 1965-66 to 1968-69 witnessed growth rates of 26, 22, 17 and 10 per cent respectively – figures which represented a complete transforma-tion of the sector. Imports of rice had been running at about two-thirds of total consumption, but now accounted for a mere 20 per cent. It was noteworthy that this striking spurt had been induced very largely by rises in the level of rice prices with complementary support from ex-tension inputs. The role of investment had been small.

Lipton's analysis based on a comparison of ICORs was sharply criticized. It was pointed out that these were prone to considerable instability and that the estimate relating to agriculture was biased strongly down-wards by the omission of the value of self-improvement work on farms and also of extension inputs. An outstanding problem was to pump more resources into agriculture and to help the poorer farmers at the same time. One view was that this was a difficult task. An opposing position held that as 50 per cent of Indian farmers were heavily in debt, a scheme which channelled credit to this group would reduce risk and stimulate innovation by lessening dependence on loans supplied by money-lenders at rates of interest of 40 per cent or more. It was also argued that the green revolution should have the effect of increasing agricultural incomes to a significant extent. Even if prices did fall, real income would rise if the extra output were consumed by the household. However, the innovation in farm practice implied by the green revolu-tion demanded extra working capital, and hence extra marketed surplus. This might preclude farmers in some very small holding categories from innovating, unless they were continually subsidized.

The third theme of the discussion was that of the role of external factors influencing Indian planning, but especially aid. One view was that there was some vagueness as to whether the projected halving of net aid by 1974 was a target or an expectation. If the former was the case, then a strong consensus of opinion inclined towards heavy criticism of the Planning Commission's proposal. Various arguments in favour of a more aid-oriented Plan were advanced. First, for India at least, the cost of doing without aid would be high. Aid accounted for about $2 *per capita* of a total of about $9 *per capita* in investment. It was highly possible that Pakistan had grown faster in recent years, not because it had better policies or development strategies, but because it had received relatively more aid. In global terms, a rational reallocation of aid should be away from Latin America and towards India— rational also because the demonstrated ability of India to use aid was good. Naturally there were political problems attendant on such a shift, due largely to India's sheer size. Yet the Planning Commission's current stance could only militate against such a shift. Secondly, and more specific to the Indian situation, India's import-intensive strategy implied that a reserve of aid would allow certain extra things to be done if all went well. On the other hand, if the course of events turned out badly and aid had been pitched rather low, then the need to obtain more aid arose. However, in view of the exceptional aid level attained during the middle and later sixties, itself the result of exceptional internal conditions during that period, one would expect aid needs to be reduced somewhat.

As a complement to this, some criticism was also levelled at aid donors on the score that, on occasion, India had been unable to absorb more aid because there had been insufficient warning by donors that aid would be forthcoming. Unhappily, there was also an obstacle on the Indian side, at least as far as the public sector was concerned: poor management ability. Finally, there was a plea that planners should not tell the people that aid was bad, and then make purposive approaches to both multilateral and bilateral donors.

Trade issues were covered almost in a footnote. The projection of a growth rate of 7 per cent in exports appeared, in one view, to be rather optimistic, especially in relation to the market prospects for tea. On the import side, the UNCTAD 'rule' that imports grew about 1 to 2 per cent faster that exports seemed to be confirmed in practice. That being the case, the Fourth Plan looked distinctly shaky on this particular issue.

Concluding the discussion, Dr Minhas declared that his task appeared to be that of replying to ten lectures. With that understood, he would do his best to cover the wide spectrum of points which had been raised.

Projections including data for years before 1950-51 were questionable on the grounds that crop-cutting techniques were not introduced until

CP2 E

that year and earlier estimates were therefore suspect. More generally, he felt compelled to make the point that statistics was a harsh discipline and that approaches based on subjective judgement were to be rejected. The only valid method was to test whether or not all the observations came from the same population. Analysis then led to two conclusions: (i) that the years 1965-66 and 1966-67 were abnormal, and (ii) that no new trend was visible after 1960-61. The projection of 4 to 4·5 per cent growth was based on likely input availabilities, and it had to be stressed that this represented a marked acceleration over the previous trend value of 3·1 per cent.[1] Moving on to the issue of the 'right' allocation to agriculture, he considered that the injection of more capital into that sector would, at this stage, produce only a small pay-off. Predictably, some people were fascinated by the table of ICORs listed in the paper; whereas the real purpose of presenting it had been to show that the Planning Commission had not computed the ICORs properly. The crux of the problem lay instead in the approach to agriculture. The right questions were not being asked and there was inadequate knowledge of quite basic factors, especially crop-water-fertilizer relationships. Until this aspect of the situation became clearer, increased allocations to agriculture would achieve relatively little.

The emergence of 55,000 unemployed engineers had triggered a shift in emphasis to primary education, but there was still an overall fall in expenditure on education from Rs. 1·15 per head per year to Rs. 0·84 indicated in the current plan. Part of the blame for this could be laid at the door of the States.

As for aid, it was true that this introduced a number of important uncertainties. However, there was still the matching problem of evolving a strategy to absorb more aid effectively. What had to be done to get more aid was also a perplexing question. In the Indian case, two or three bouts of increases in taxation had not caused any extra aid to materialize.

[1] In the period 1950-51 to 1964-65, the trend rate of growth of output in agriculture was about 3·1 per cent. The drought years of 1965-66 and '66-67 were quite abnormal on the strict statistical grounds that those observations fell outside 5 per cent confidence limits. The estimating relation which had been used was of the form

$$P_0 e^{rt} = A_0 e^{r_1 t} \, Y_0 e^{r_2 t} \, C_0 e^{r_3 t}$$

where P_0, A_0, Y_0 and C_0 represented production, gross crop area, yield and cropping pattern respectively, all measured in the base year; r, r_1, r_2, and r_3 were the trend (logarithmic) rates of growth corresponding to the above variables. Analysis revealed that there was no new overall trend in evidence after the close of the 1950s.

As regards political prospects, it was quite pernicious to argue that because India had been stable in the past, it would continue to be so in the future. Increasing the incomes of the already employed was not important compared with generating incomes for the presently unemployed. A stepping-up of the growth rate of GDP from 5 to 7 per cent per annum would not diminish the destitute fractile to the lowest tenth. In the absence of such radical measures, what had happened in Pakistan could very well be repeated in India–only on a much fiercer scale.

Planning the Improvement of Planning in India and Pakistan

Group Report,[1] *by* Michael Lipton

A. The Context and its Relevance to Planning

At least since 1958 in Pakistan and from 1951 to 1964 in India, the medium-term plans have been serious documents, designed to be implemented, and not destroyed by 'political competition' (see pp. 58-60) though threatened by centrifugal tendencies. Planned resource allocations have stimulated regional, departmental and other rivalries; they have also helped to unify each country by formalizing and organizing its regions' dependence on central funds, experts and foreign exchange.[2] Since 1966 India has proceeded with very loose annual plans and some sector programming, but only shadowy medium-term plans. The latest annual plan (1969-70) was closely linked to the budget, and to the emerging 1969-74 Indian Plan; this tries to incorporate checks and flexibility by envisaging annual plans too. In Pakistan, annual planning began to support the five-year frame two years ago.

India (540 million people) and Pakistan (125 million) have together a population exceeding that of Africa and Latin America combined. Income-per-head in the two countries is about the same, about £20 per person per year – almost the lowest in the world,[3] with severe and probably growing regional and rural-urban inequality, such that the worse-off half of populations get only about £10 per person per year. The continental size and diversity of both countries invalidates many *overall* comparisons; growth in the Punjab compares favourably, in Bihar unfavourably, with growth almost anywhere. Pakistan is divided into two regions, separated by Indian territory; West Pakistan is much less poor

---

[1] Amended after plenary discussion.

[2] Even if, as in Pakistan, the Centre obtained these resources by directly exploiting one or other of its regions.

[3] On p. 48, Dr Minhas shows that even an almost incredible growth performance in India – 5½ per cent per year till 1985 – will leave one in ten Indians destitute. The Pakistan Perspective Plan projects growth rising from 6 per cent to 8 per cent by 1985; Dr Papanek estimates that, if this very rapid rate were achieved, Pakistan would by 1985 reach Egyptian income-per-head of 1959.

than East. Indian States differ in poverty, language, industrialization, and loyalty to Congress and to Delhi.

The great variety of resources, however sparse, in such huge countries implies a smaller reliance on foreign trade than in most of the under-developed world; exports have been typically 4 to 6 per cent of GNP, but imports, under the strains of development, have grown to 8 to 10 per cent. How can the gap be filled? Private capital inflow seldom exceeds profit repatriation; there have been since 1957 few reserves of foreign exchange to run down; that leaves aid. Net aid finances a much larger share of Pakistan's investment than of India's.

These countries' great poverty inhibits private saving, but India in particular – partly because more industrialized by 1950 – has achieved a high marginal savings rate since. However, the final uses of savings in India, as in Pakistan until about 1962, have not followed Plan priorities. The private sector has transformed its savings into private investments (often to make highly protected, and in India low-priority, consumer goods), rather than being taxed to finance a pattern of investment conforming to plan priorities. To remedy this tendency, Pakistan has switched increasingly to selective incentives to approved private investment; India has preferred licensing policies. The difference has been less in ideology (Pakistan's public-sector share in total investment is higher than India's) than in strategy and initial situation; Pakistan, with her smaller manufacturing sector in 1950, has concentrated less on building up heavy industry, and more on private-sector *consumer-goods* exports and import-substitutes, than India. In general, however, both countries' plans have shown bogus symmetry, presenting side-by-side sectoral allocations for public and private sectors under circumstances where inadequate controls existed to implement the latter. The public sector now accounts for about half of gross investment in both countries.

Indian and Pakistan planners' control over the private sector is complicated by the countries' economic structure. In both countries, now as in 1951, about 70 per cent of workers are employed in agriculture, producing only 45 per cent of GNP, partly because endowed with only 20-25 per cent of capital stock and even smaller shares of skilled workers. The mass of economic agents are scattered in villages of 400-800 persons, offering great difficulties of administration and overview. Even indirect controls (such as price policies) have quite different effects on different regions, in ways hard to predict. Both countries have experimented with different administrative systems for the rural sector, often cutting confusingly across each other, but contributing the first stages of a possibly inevitable search process: search for a system reconciling the central authorities' wish to control with their need to decentralize.

At least Indian and Pakistani planners deal with settled, nucleated villagers. Another advantage over some less developed countries is their greater endowment of highly trained civil servants, statisticians, and engineers (the latter in substantial surplus in India). Recently – and partly because of earlier Plan decisions – shortages of major groups of professional persons have seldom been the binding constraints in planned growth, although misallocations (doctors to urban private practices), inappropriate training (in centralized agricultural colleges) and wrong composition (insufficiently specialized accountants and engineers) have been serious problems.

Both India and Pakistan, then, face an environment for planning economically hopeful in respect of civil-service and manpower endowment and (if only by contrast with most countries in Africa and Latin America) immunity from trade trends and fluctuations.[1] They are, however, more threatened by the separatist consequences of great size, and much more prone to acute land scarcity as populations grow. Neither country has yet evolved a serious employment *policy*, although chapters on the subject appear regularly in plans; yet workforces are growing by $2\frac{1}{2}$-3 per cent yearly, industry fast but at very high capital/labour ratios, and farmland to work hardly at all. Fortunately the 'new strategy' in agriculture, at least at first, is employment-generating. East Pakistan's rural works policy has had some success – by paying employees adequate wages – since 1965.

Both countries have tried to mobilize political support for development. In both, the mobilizing machinery (Pakistan's 'basic democracies', India's CD and panchayati raj, etc.) has been inefficient or captured by traditional ruling groups or both. But in both countries most economic agents, including peasants, have been highly responsive to opportunities to raise profits and wages. A serious attempt to share these opportunities more equally might represent the planners' best chance to mobilize popular support (especially insofar as the 'savings' generated by inequality often find their way into low-priority investment).

B. Planning Office and Organization

In both countries, the top-level planning body comprises mainly senior politicians and administrators. In India this body takes sub-

---

[1] The dependence of their strategy on imports, especially of raw materials, has nevertheless meant that small foreign-exchange shortfalls have serious development effects.

stantive decisions about the bulk of the Plan; the second level of authority in the Planning Commission comprises senior advisers, also administrators; the research staff are at the third level; but the expertise of the Perspective Planning Division, and recent elevations to the Commission itself, have given the technicians more prestige. In Pakistan the politicians are a formal body only; the real decisions within the Planning Commission are taken by the economists.

Further differences concern the power of the Planning Commission. *Vis-à-vis political leadership*, the Pakistan Commission, after Ayub's initial disregard in 1958, were able to convince him that they could give competent advice, acceptance of which paid political dividends, and Ayub in turn saw to it that the Commission gained strength; but the years of Ayub's declining power (1967-69) also saw the Commission in decline. In India, Nehru (and to a lesser extent his successors) favoured planning, but were less able to break up 'administrative feudalism' and give the Commission real power, largely because India is more democratic and less authoritarian, but partly because the successes of planning came slowly and were resisted by the business community, whereas the main beneficiaries of Pakistani planning – entrepreneurs and big farmers – also provided the main political support for Ayub.

Vis-à-vis regional authorities, Pakistani politicians largely suppressed them, making planning easier but risking an explosion. In India, the National Development Council (of State Chief Ministers), which must approve Central Plans, have become more than a lobby against State fund-raising and for Central assistance. There are two parts of Indian public-sector plan outlays, Central and State. Central outlays, largely in industry and infra-structure, are rather more than half the total. About half the State outlays are supported by Centrally-raised tax funds, and the National Development Council has agreed on a formula for allocating these among States. Since 1965 this is done by block grants, not project-tied funds, though Commission approval is still needed for major projects. State-level planning is still primitive, and Commission efforts are centred on allocating funds among *sectors*, though its Working Parties engage in several rounds of discussion with States. India's increasing decentralization of planning to the States weakens Central authority and planning rationality, but recognizes the changing balance of power.

Vis-à-vis local authorities, both countries have tried to secure 'participation' and 'planning from below' by various means. At levels below District (1½-2½ million people) these have not been very successful.

Cumbersome, time-consuming, dominated by big farmers, they have at least improved liaison between local civil servants and informal village leaders.

Vis-à-vis the *Ministry of Finance*, the Indian Planning Commission have been losing more and more battles; the Pakistan Commission supported by an authoritarian but highly rational state machine, have been winning. The Pakistan Commission's power is due partly to their direct control of aid funds; the Indian Commission's advice on the uses of non-project aid is sometimes rejected by the Finance Ministry. The Pakistan Commission planners have sometimes been more important than the Finance Ministry in annual budget-making; not so in India. Indian planning is delayed by a rather cumbersome process under which, for each Plan, a *separate* 'Finance Commission' effectively shares power to project fund-raising with the planners.

Vis-à-vis operational ministries and public corporations, both Commissions face frustrating conflicts. Public financial auditing (through the Comptroller and Auditor-General) is largely negative, discouraging imaginative decisions by officials; there is no proper Commission 'performance audit' in ministries or corporations, to see what month-to-month progress is being made on Plan projects. Evaluation Commissions, Mid-term Appraisals, etc., have been poor substitutes for prompt check-ups and access to information.

Vis-à-vis private business, policies have been spelt out only in very general terms. Targets have been related only loosely to incentives. Partly this is inevitable (flexibility is needed, and businessmen forewarned about policies may be forearmed to frustrate them); but in some respects, in particular the chronic underpricing of public-utility outputs for private business, the lack of a thought-through policy to reconcile private and public output targets has been unnecessary and damaging. Both countries have moved towards increasing use of deliberate price *policy* (not the 'price mechanism') to achieve Plan goals, especially in agriculture.[1] Pakistan moved first, but less far than is often thought (cf. the rising share of investment under direct public control). Pakistan's use of price incentives in foreign-exchange management – if the IMF would permit – could be considered in India (it was actually set back by India's 'bonfire of controls' accompanying devaluation). Price incentives work, but nobody really knows how fast, or how far, or how combined with unintended incentives from local or temporary demand-

[1] Cf. G. Papanek, *Pakistan's Development: Social Goals and Private Incentives*, Cambridge, Mass. 1967, esp. Ch. VIII.

supply imbalances (e.g. at harvest time). The new planning orthodoxy of Incentives and Inputs has militated against proper attention to rural institutions (rural banks, labour exchanges, etc.) needed to help market incentives to work. In the industrial sector, Indian planners are doubtful if pricing can really replace licensing as a control on entry in a *planned* industrial structure; buffer stocks, implementable plans for priority sectors, and controllable raw-material imports are seen as pre-requisites for an inevitably slow relaxation of direct controls. It is generally admitted in India that effective licensing without effective anti-monopoly policy has produced increasing and probably undesirable concentration of economic power.

In both countries, the main operational document has been the Five-year Plan, though India has had a three-year interregnum (1966-7 – 1968-9) with Annual Plans only. Both countries have draft plans, published for discussion and parliamentary approval before a final plan appears. The draft plans have always been published too late, and characteristically plans have got under way with only project documents finalised. The planning model in both countries involves specifying a final bill of goods to be consumed, invested and exported by the last year of the plan; using input-output analysis to find the intermediate goods needed to make this final bill of goods; working out the investment needed to make these goods; seeing if savings plus aid could be raised to finance this investment; and, if not, adjusting proposals for the final bill of goods and/or the savings effort until a consistent plan emerged. There are several weaknesses in the model-building effort, spelt out below.

C. Weaknesses and Remedies

1. *Incomplete planning model*

This is considered first only for continuity, not because it is the most serious weakness. The main problem here is poor specification of the final bill of goods. The 'required' extra outputs of some items (e.g. foodgrain types) are obtained by multiplying the expected growth of incomes of main groups of consumers by their income-elasticities of demand, so that income distributions are assumed given and costly milk is scheduled to replace cheap pulses as a protein source, while technical change favouring particular crops gets insufficient weight *vis-à-vis* expected demand shifts. Some outputs are arbitrarily projected to grow as fast as population; some, to meet targets (e.g. for number of villages to be electrified) specified exogenously without proper estimation of costs and benefits; some (for goods that can be consumed *or* invested), to fill gaps in Material Balance projections. Over-reliance on standard input-output has drawbacks too – neglect of non-linearities and hence too-small cement and caustic-soda plants,[1] linear contingency 'planning', too little attention to technical change. As for the relations between needed outputs (final and intermediate) and new investment, shortfalls have been too often met by downward fudging of capital output ratios, especially for regions (like East Pakistan) where growth was sought without the will to allocate enough resources. The remedy for all this is not a return to 'intuitive planning' but more realistic models, based on the relations between inputs and outputs actually prevailing, not on linear assumptions.

2. *Data deficiencies*

The right data must be collected for any improvement in the Plan models, or (even more important) in the planners' ability to see if plans are being implemented. Lack of data about project returns and risks have reduced the yield from plan projects.[2] Plenty of excess data are already being gathered – it is a matter of reassigning statisticians, especially at State (Province) level, from useless routine work to the prompt publication of data needed for plans. Such data should be promptly passed to greatly strengthened Project Evaluation and Control sections in the Planning Commissions. Short-run data – prices, production, balance of payments – are essential ammunition if the Commissions are to protect long-run objectives. Another data deficiency is that the response of farmers and small businessmen to alternative incentives is grossly under-researched. Education and health priorities are assessed on vague social criteria and/or highly aggregative frames, instead of analyses of the *effects* of alternative outlays on alternative desiderata. All this adds up to the need to gear data collection much more to project evaluation–*vis-à-vis* all plan aims, including employment and equalisation as well as growth.

3. *Vulnerability and over-optimism.*

This combination is dangerous. Bits of the plan depend on each other; over-optimism in one sector can mean serious waste elsewhere.

---

[1] Alan S. Manne, ed., *Investments for Capacity Expansion*, Cambridge, Mass. 1967, p. 142.

[2] See P. Streeten and M. Lipton, ed., *The Crisis of Indian Planning*, Oxford 1968, pp. 7-10.

Over-optimism often takes the form of ignoring vulnerability to risk. The three most serious sources of risk are crop fluctuations, exports earnings, and aid receipts. In the last case, donors are playing a self-defeating game, switching pledged aid on and off in a way that seriously reduces its yield.[1] Both India and Pakistan need contingency plans: not just linear models that say 'if aid and private savings show 10 per cent shortfalls then cut all investment 10 per cent', but reassessments of priorities in the light of risks. There is a case for a 'core plan', as in India in 1957 but prepared in advance, that will *not* be given up. In preparing core and contingency plans, detailed knowledge of inter-sectoral relations is needed. Another approach is to compare the costs and benefits of *alternative* ways of sacrificing growth to safety: invest-ments to cut risks, e.g. irrigation; investments to concentrate output in low-risk areas, e.g. fertilizers for areas with irrigation already; and invest-ments to lessen the effects of bad luck, e.g. buffer stocks. Another requirement is project-specific cut-off rules, related both to inadequate yields and to possible shortfalls in supply or demand for the project; here again, the Commission *must* be in touch with short-run changes, or ministries will decide the *de facto* core plan. If all this presents too great political or administrative difficulties, there is a strong case for 'built-in stabilizers' as incorporated in Pakistan's export bonus voucher scheme.

4. *Failure to quantify aims and choose among them.*

Objectives have been stated without serious thought as to their reconciliation. Hence growth of real GNP, being both relatively easy to measure and the centre of many current economic models, has been emphasized, and other crucial aims, especially employment, tacked on as afterthoughts. The effect of industrialization or a big-farm strategy – themselves not always openly stated – on employment and equality has not been worked out. Plans are political documents and cannot be expected to expose fully their own shortcomings. But political documents that are all things to all men, on the one hand – on the other hand, where all policies secure all aims – these merely breed cynicism. In the 'political competition' the Plan has little chance if it does not seem to be rational. In particular, employment in India and equalisation in Pakistan must come much nearer to the quantitative centre of planning.

---

[1] The group met too early to discuss the question of aid diverted to arms used for civil repression in East Bengal. In those circumstances, I judge, the group would have unanimously disapproved of the continuance of aid.

5. *Belief in the 'power of the word'*[1]

This has meant long delays in recognition that proclaimed policies
–CD, co-operative farms, some aspects of local democratization – have
been expensive failures. It has also caused relative neglect of implementation – cf. the long delay before under-utilisation of irrigation was
even recognized as a planning problem. Where 'action not words' has
been sought, adherence to plan orthodoxies has been far weaker – the
rapid switch in family planning, from IUDs to sterilization, illustrates.

6. *Inadequate public-sector financing*

'Gaps to be filled by new/higher taxes', between planned public
outlays and expected public revenues, and in excess of 'permissible
deficit finance', have been regular features of both countries' planning.
Partly this is because of constitutional and expectational needs not to
disclose tax plans; partly, especially in India, it has reflected (*a*) un-
realism in the Commission about what taxes could be raised, (*b*) inadequate 'teeth' in the Commission to get States and Finance Ministry to
bring in the money. By the standards of post-war world inflation, neither
India nor Pakistan has had severe long-term price rises; unscheduled
gaps have been met by public investment shortfalls, not severe inflation.
These shortfalls have particularly affected the rural sector.

7. *Economism*

More specific attention to aims other than growth is needed. The
structure of power, especially in villages, should be more consciously
used – or changed – to generate progress. Rural and other sociological
knowledge, already available, should be quantified where possible and
incorporated into the process of planning.

8. *Absence of proper decentralization*

(*a*) *Areas.* A greater emphasis on planning *within* poor regions – East
Pakistan, Bihar – may help correct the regional inequalities produced by
growth; the hypercentralizing formula of 'growth now, equality later' is
not viable politically. In Pakistan, properly staffed and responsible
planning bodies at Province level may be needed to prevent an explosion.
In India, enormous resources under States' control – financed largely by
united 'block grants' from the Centre – are in great need of proper State
planning, though there is room for disagreement about how to link this

---

[1] Cf. A. H. Hanson, *The Process of Planning*, Oxford 1966, *passim*.

to the Planning Commission at the Centre. In both countries, decentralization below District level has had very little success, and should give way to District attempts to produce departmental co-ordination and some degree of popular participation.

(b) *Enterprises.* In the *private* sector attempts to control firms by licensing and physical allocation have often proved in the context of 'the soft State'[1] ineffective, corruptible, administratively costly, and above all productive of the very inequality and concentration of power they sought to prevent; indirect controls, via price policy, may sometimes be less inegalitarian as well as more efficient. *Public* enterprises in both countries have been hamstrung by a colonial legacy of purely negative controls on spending and thus on initiative; in particular the functions of the Comptroller and Auditor-General should be drastically revised.

9. *Ministerial training*

Lack of appropriate *training* is not a problem within the Planning Commissions themselves, although they might make more use of the micro-level knowledge, the *quantified* sociological data, and the rural specialisms already available in their own countries. India, indeed, is a net exporter of economists and statisticians. Yet both (like the UK) lack these specialisms within the *Ministries* (except the Finance Ministry). Such documents as the Report of the Indian Education Commission, for all their merits, have little bearing on the plan priorities or frameworks. Economic training for officials, in the Ministries at Centre and State level, is needed to improve Planning Commission-administrator liaison. Except for a handful of institutions, economics training and textbooks in India and Pakistan do not encourage original applied work – problem-oriented hypothesis testing in a local context – relevant to planning.

10. *Co-operation in the South Asian region*

Finally, institutions of *regional planning* are needed, though high-level personnel should not be taken from their desks unless there is a good chance that action will result. In *trade expansion*, duplication risks might be considered by joint teams, especially in textiles; even hostile countries could collaborate here. In *agricultural planning*, are the region's cereal producers learning from each other? And are they in

[1] G. Myrdal, *Asian Drama*, New York, 1968, Vol. I, p. 66; Vol. II, pp. 895-900.

danger of replacing each other's exports, for little joint benefit? Even in *defence planning*, versions of 'arms control agreements' might reduce the share of GNP that India and Pakistan at present devote to preparations for conflict. As for *international capital flows*, meetings of World Bank consortia and ADB *might* turn out better for both India and Pakistan if potential capital sources could be convinced that their plans had been aligned to prevent duplication. None of these possibilities need wait upon a political settlement in Kashmir or Bengal.

Chapter Two

THE LESSONS OF EXPERIENCE: ASIA

Dr P. S. N. Prasad[1]

The problems of economic development and planning in Asia were dramatized in 1968 by the publication of Gunnar Myrdal's *Asian Drama*, which is a monumental study in many ways, but suffers from a temptation to generalize in relation to the problems of an area as large and varied as Asia.

A few months after the publication of *Asian Drama*, an article in *Life*[2] magazine presented some facts about real GNP *per capita* in thirty-two countries from Africa, Asia, Australia, Europe and the Americas. Although it was aimed largely at laymen rather than at professional economists, and related to economic growth in 1968 only, this article depicted a situation rather different from the somewhat unrelieved gloom of Myrdal's *Asian Drama*.

Out of the thirty-two countries listed, two countries from Asia had the highest growth rates in that year, *viz.*, Japan and Taiwan. Among the first seven countries with the highest growth rates, five were from Asia–Japan, Taiwan, South Korea, Iran and Thailand. To these should be added Singapore and Hong Kong, although these were not given in the chart. Some of the Asian countries which have taken seriously to economic planning according to theories of development taken from the experience of Western countries, like Pakistan and India, did not have growth rates comparable with those of the Asian countries mentioned above, and India ranks thirtieth in a list of thirty-two countries. According to other evidence (not in the *Life* charts), these dynamic five or seven in Asia mentioned above also enjoyed (*a*) reasonable price stability, (*b*) satisfactory rates of growth in exports, (*c*) fairly sound balance

---

[1] This paper was written by Dr Prasad when he was Director of the UN Asian Institute for Economic Development in Bangkok. The views expressed are his personal views and not those of any organizations with which he is professionally connected.

[2] *Life*, Asian edn., 11 Nov. 1968.

of payments positions, and (*d*) excellent records of resource mobilization, domestic and foreign, which sustained their appreciable growth rates.

I think it would be useful to reflect on these divergent patterns of the development picture in Asia – which to some extent belie the easy generalization that Asian attitudes and institutions make it difficult to organize rapid economic development and modernization of the structures of production and distribution.

The first point to be made about the Asian economic development situation is that there is not just one Asia – the Asia of Myrdal's drama – but at least three types of Asia that one can observe – segments which, in many significant ways, are different from each other. First, the Asia which, with little trumpeting and fanfare about economic planning and without much serious effort at macro-planning, has achieved considerable success in development and modernization. There is another segment of countries, of which India and Pakistan are representative, which have taken to sophisticated planning techniques, but have achieved less conspicuous results on the whole. Lastly, there is a third segment of countries which are close to economic stagnation. Myrdal's analysis, in my view, is based rather largely on the experience of the second segment and tends to generalize on that basis for the whole of Asia. *I suggest that the less successful of the Asian countries have a lot to learn from the experience of the more successful group, even more, perhaps, than they have to gain by drawing from the ideology and techniques of the industrialized Western countries.*

There is sometimes an argument advanced that the success of some of the South-East Asian economies which have done well during the last few years is due to the large-scale *per capita* economic aid given to them and the growth of business opportunities arising from the Vietnam war. This observation is not without an element of truth in it. But the fact that when opportunities are available, the country's entrepreneurs are able and willing to take advantage of them is really the more relevant point. That Thailand, Taiwan, and South Korea have done so, and that Cambodia, Burma, Indonesia, and even India have not done so, is also relevant. Even foreign aid, if not made use of productively, would have engendered only inflation and economic distortions. That this has not happened only redounds to the credit of these countries and underlines the fact that enterprise and production have responded to the flow of funds in ways which have assisted the growth of these economies.

The experience of Japan fully refutes the Myrdal doctrine that the

Asian attitudes and institutions are an obstacle to economic development and social change. Japan, which remains dedicated to its native
traditions and institutions, has been able to produce all the necessary
flexibility to transform itself into a most modern economic machine. It
has borrowed heavily from Western technology and successfully grafted
it onto its own institutional and organizational patterns. Unlike India,
it did not take to Western ideologies of the welfare state and trade
unionism at the very start of its development career, though it is moving
cautiously and realistically towards these social goals after perfecting
the growth of its productive apparatus. It has nothing to regret for its
heavy reliance on private industry and, in my view, represents a model
for a country like India, where the debate on the efficacy of the public,
as opposed to the private sector, has assumed the proportions of a
religious debate based on faith rather than facts. Although Japan has
its socialists and even communists, it has managed to retain an exem-
plary harmony between labour, capital, and management, unlike India,
where the bitter cleavage between labour and management remains a
great obstacle to the growth of the economy at its full potential. Japan
had not seriously taken to macro-planning, and yet growth projections
produced by the Japanese economic planning agency frequently fell far
short of the actual achievements of its entrepreneurs, farmers and
industrial workers. By and large, Japan did not organize its economic
growth on the basis of economic development theories absorbed from
the West, and its ancient social traditions yielded enough, as each occasion demanded, to make possible the absorption of technology needed
to make the next steps in economic advancement. Above all, in spite of
its conspicuous success on the production front, the Japanese worker
still remains a model of incessant industry, particularly for his counter-
part in many Asian countries.

In Taiwan, as in Japan, the key to rapid growth lies in the enormous
industry of its people. A small island, full of rocky soil, it has been
transformed into a veritable garden, with a record of success in agricultural achievement without a parallel anywhere else in Asia. This tiny
island has now been persuaded to send over three thousand agricultural
technicians and demonstrators to several countries in Africa and Asia
which are anxious to profit by its experience. It has developed a most
successful tourist industry and has, in collaboration particularly with
Japan and the United States, developed an excellent base for manufacturing industries geared substantially to export promotion. Labour-
management relations are remarkably harmonious and there is little

evidence of irresponsible and negative trade unionism, or of resistance to social and economic change from fossilized behavioural patterns. Its people have responded constructively to economic incentives and opportunities, and policy-making has remained largely pragmatic and flexible. Both project planning and planning in the promising sectors have been meticulously cautious, and although they have not yet taken to macro-planning, they are now making earnest efforts in that direction.

Thailand is another economy which has shown a remarkable capacity for economic growth in recent years. It has taken to some kind of flexible macro-planning, but has made a success of many of its individual projects and sectoral developments in irrigation and power. Although long associated with the west in its political leanings and economic ambitions, it has retained a great deal of its own traditional and institutional patterns, accepting technology, but remaining faithful to the native tradition and philosophy wherever feasible, and accepting change where necessary with imperceptible adaptations. It has relied heavily on private enterprise and opened the gates wide for the flow of private capital, know-how, and technical skills, and has up to now not felt any reason to regret the offer of such freedoms. Its financial management has been sober and conservative, and it has accumulated the largest *per capita* foreign exchange reserves in all of Asia. It has certain elements of unevenness in its development strategy and a lack of sufficient attention to the proper policies of distribution, but these have not proved a serious problem in the context of a rapid, overall growth of the economy, and the labour-capital relations on the whole remains harmonious. There is little serious resistance to social change deemed desirable for economic betterment, even though the general fabric of behaviour reflects a traditional and conservative bias.

In my judgement, all these three countries, together with South Korea, constitute a solid refutation of Myrdal's dramatic doctrines. Some of them still have their weaknesses and limitations, but these are not serious enough to stem the growing pace of economic progress. Some of them have serious political problems and problems of security, but given an escape from these, they will in fact achieve dramatic results both in economic development and modernization.

India's economic planning differs from that of the countries described above in its approaches and attitudes. As both the world's largest democracy and poorest country, it has, quite appropriately, in some ways, kept in the centre of all its plan activities the question of social and distributive justice. This is both its strength and its weakness. It is its strength because the Indian planners will perhaps never invite an attack on the ground that the economic development of the country is being left in the hands of twenty families, though the communists in India still assail the government in spite of this excessive emphasis on distributive justice. Its weakness lies in the fact that the policies of the Indian Government have tended by and large to support labour, which has produced a great deal of indiscipline in industry, both in the public and the private sectors (but much more so in the public sector), and have tended to place management at a serious disadvantage in day-to-day business *vis-à-vis* labour. This has made the job of management in the industrial sector an increasingly unattractive one. In view of India's great shortage of managerial talent, such policies are proving to be a serious handicap to Indian economic growth.

Indian planning is full of idealism and compassion, but it remains yet to be seen as to how realistic it is. India, and in almost similar measure, Pakistan, are probably the two countries in Asia which have drawn heavily on the ideas of western industrialized societies, and in particular from the British trade unionists and the British Labour Party. Generations of Indian intellectuals have grown up under the intellectual spell of Laski, Pigou, Beveridge and Keynes, and have taken to humanistic ideas of socialism and welfare economics to an extent which is not seen in other Asian countries, except, perhaps, Ceylon and Malaysia.

The welfare ideas implanted in the native idealism of Indian philosophy and temperament created in the mind of Indian planners the vision of achieving a welfare state simultaneously with, if not even ahead of, the establishment of an economic and industrial base which is necessary to sustain it. Within the framework of this philosophy, India has produced three successive macro-plans, and after a gap of about three years, is now engaged in forging a fourth plan. Throughout much of this period the planners have scrupulously kept aloof from the views of Indian businessmen and industrialists, unlike Japan, where the government, businessmen, and labour interests have generally forged a harmonious approach to tackling Japan's economic development. This distance which the Indian planners keep from Indian businessmen is again both a strength and a weakness – a strength in that the planners keep themselves away from being 'tainted' by contact with business houses, a position which looks good in the eyes of the vast, impoverished populace of India – and a weakness because few of the planners in India are people who could provide the wisdom that comes from practical

experience in handling any sizeable economic jobs in business or industry, even though they are excellent professionals in their own chosen
fields.

Perhaps for this reason, while India's macro-planning looks respect-
able in terms of economic concepts and statistical models, it remains
weak in its sectoral planning, and disastrously weak in the planning of
its projects, in particular the ones in the public sector. According to
information released by the government up to about 1968, of fifty-five
enterprises in the public sector, thirty-one have made a total gain of
Rs. 480 million, while twenty-four units have incurred losses of Rs.
830 million, thus showing an overall loss on a total investment of Rs.
32,000 million.

Making their plans employment- and welfare-oriented, India's
planners have paid less attention to the strict needs and criteria of
production, and these policies have resulted in an average growth rate
for the total plan period that only slightly exceeded population growth
during the same period. It is, of course, ultimately a matter of political
choice as to whether a country opts for a rapid growth of production,
as in Japan, South Korea, Taiwan and Thailand, with social justice
following, or for a more stable democratic society which moves forward
very slowly or even remains close to economic stagnation. In the last
analysis, the economist is not competent to deliver judgement on what
should be the appropriate choice between such alternatives, but it can
certainly be said by the economist that Indian planning is weighted
heavily by the rigidities of socialism and welfare economics, and a
number of minor ones like prohibition, cow protection, and so on.
Indian planning has also frowned on the earning of profit beyond what
is considered a 'reasonable' measure, and this has, by and large, tended
to discourage and restrict enterprise and risk-taking. Placing a profound
faith in the virtues of public enterprise, it has resorted to nationalization
of insurance and certain sectors of commercial banking. In both cases,
costs have since risen and efficiency has come down. It has invested
heavily in developing an industrial base that ignored some of the important criteria of sound investment and economic management.

In respect of a great deal of labour legislation that has been passed
since independence, as well as measures of nationalization for central
and commercial banking and insurance, and in matters relating to industrial licensing and policies under discussion for the disbursement of
commercial credits, the planners in India seem to be concerned rather
largely with problems of distributive justice. They are apparently in-

different to the impact of these policies on efficient and economical production, on enterprise, on incentives and on innovative ideas. If confronted by such a charge, they would probably protest that this is not the case. One can only surmise that either they do not have much appreciation of the mechanics and the motivations of production, or that in a democracy it is considered politically expedient to concentrate attention on the distributive needs of the economy, no matter what its cost may be in terms of efficient production or economic growth.

Placing great faith in controls and licensing as ways of securing the best possible allocations, Indian planners have imposed physical and financial controls at so many points in the economy that a whole army of administrators is busy getting in each other's way and adding a great deal of confusion and delay to the day-to-day operations of enterprise both public and private.

The most serious problem in Indian planning remains, however, in runaway trade unionism which is fostered to some extent by the well-meaning bias of the Indian planners in favour of social justice, and to some extent also by the substantial dependence of political leaders on labour votes. The political and union leaders of today find it difficult to curb these trends, in spite of their largely negative and destructive contribution. There are few in India today who are able to stand up to the recurring demands of labour, or able to impress on them an appreciation of the relation between productivity and wages.

A country like India, with its great size and population, together with the complexities of caste loyalty and linguistic awareness, cannot be compared with Thailand, Taiwan, or even Japan, all of which are happily free from many of its more intractable problems. Nevertheless, their recent experience refutes the generalized assertions concerning Asia which were made by Myrdal. Their growth rates have been splendid; they have been responsive to the needs of modernization, not only in the large urban centres, but even in the rural sector; they have tolerated and developed a great deal of private initiative and enterprise; they have shown themselves capable of making pragmatic and realistic assessments of their economic needs and opportunities; but above all, they have managed to keep their populations working hard and industriously, while largely maintaining harmony between national and sectional interests. It is true that high growth rates are not identical with development that would ensure social and political stability in the longer run. Yet who can assert that a high rate of growth is not also a necessary condition for the creation of an economic base for social contentment?

Other Asian countries, and even non-Asian developing countries, no doubt await with interest the results of these divergent approaches to economic policy – idealistic, welfare-oriented planning on the one side, and the severely pragmatic, growth-oriented policy-making on the other.

AFRICA

Chapter Three

PLANNING IN TANZANIA

DR BRIAN VAN ARKADIE

TANZANIA is of interest partly because it is typical – an export-orientated, agrarian, low income economy quite similar in economic structure and social development to many African countries – if anything poorer and less developed than most. Tanzania is of special interest, however, because its response to the development problem has been atypical. Since independence in 1961 a developmental strategy has been emerging which is likely to have considerable appeal in other parts of Africa, and the success or failure of which will be a critical influence on the pattern of development throughout Africa.

The First Five-Year Plan was ambitious in its targets and implied a serious commitment to development. In detail, however, it emphasized dependence on external financial support and failed to reflect all the implications of the rural nature of Tanzanian society. Moreover, although the Plan was in principle comprehensive, much of the economy was dominated by external influences which were only in small part susceptible to influence by available policy instruments. Not only was the economy heavily dependent on external trade, and therefore primary commodity markets, but much of the 'modern' economy (e.g. banking, insurance, industry) was foreign-owned, while a significant segment of exports was produced on foreign owned estates. The available policy tools largely consisted of fiscal policy (at the outset of the Plan even monetary policy was largely passive under the Currency Board system) and development programmes in the traditional areas of central government concern (e.g. education, agricultural extension, roads).

Implementation achievements and growth performance were, by some standards, satisfactory, although falling short of the objectives set in the Plan. Nevertheless, the limited development options open in light of the degree of external dependence became increasingly evident. Also, it became clear that the pursuit of apparently neutral 'developmental' objectives led to the creation of a capitalist society and a dual economy. As a result there was a sharp change in strategy, introduced in the Arusha Declaration of February, 1967. The Arusha Declaration, and the steps taken to implement it, transformed the institutional setting and redefined the society's objectives, creating the need for a quite different kind of planning.

Criteria for Judgement

There are a number of conceptual difficulties involved in evaluating plan performance:

(i) The success of development planning can only be judged against the *objectives* pursued. It is a commonplace that a simple index of growth, such as *per capita* GDP, rarely incorporates all the objectives a society sets itself. Nevertheless, although this is usually recognized in *principle*, much discussion of planning in practice judges performance against supposedly 'neutral' output indicators. In the Tanzanian case this would be most unsatisfactory in light of the multiplicity of objectives explicitly stated in planning documents and implicit in the political environment.

(ii) *Development* planning must be judged by its long-term effects, as much as by performance in, for example, a given plan period. Development will only be achieved over many decades, if not generations.

(iii) Performance under planning must be judged, at least in part, against some view of what would have happened in the absence of plans. On the one hand, even if plan targets are not achieved the plan may have had considerable positive impact on performance. On the other hand, much growth which took place in the recent plan period would have happened, plan or no plan. If a target is achieved as a result of good or lucky (or cautious) prediction, it cannot be concluded that the prediction *caused* the achievement. (An obvious point, but again often forgotten in practice.)

(iv) If plan operation is to be judged against some ideal model of plan procedure, then that ideal must be relevant to ideal circumstances. The 'best' model for US (or USSR) conditions will not be the best model for Tanzania. Planners often recognise this point when evaluating projects; the point is also relevant to plans and planning procedure.

(v) When we are evaluating Tanzanian planning, are we considering *the Five-Year Plan*, or the planning process in which the plan document is an incident? Much recent discussion of Tanzanian planning has concentrated on the First Five-Year Plan document. In fact, of course, the success of planning depends on the degree to which the process extends beyond the Plan document and, indeed, the Planning Ministry.

Organization of Planning

Evolution of planning in Tanzania followed a course similar to that in other ex-British colonies in Africa. Some first steps were made during the colonial period. Following the Second World War (and the passage of the Colonial Development and Welfare Act), a ten-year development and welfare plan was published in 1946 (and revised in 1950). During the 1950s there was the East African Royal Commission Report (1953-1955), followed by a Five-Year Development Plan (1955) which was subsequently revised (1957) following surveys of education, agricultural and medical services. In 1959, just before independence, there was a World Bank Economic Survey Mission, which presented a substantial report in 1960. Following the Mission report, in 1961, a Three-Year Development Plan was launched.

The First Five-Year Plan of the post-independence period (1964-69) attempted a major extension in planning, providing targets for all sub-sectors, both for output and investment. The Plan was comprehensive in the sense that a view was incorporated of the role to be played by all parts of the economy.

At the time of formulation of the First Plan a Directorate of Planning was established. It was placed in the President's office and given wide-ranging powers. Initially, it was started with a small international team of planners who were responsible for formulating the First Plan. Following the Plan publication this team broke up, and for a period the Directorate suffered from lack of staff. In 1966 the Directorate was moved from the President's office and became a separate ministry. Since then the Tanzanian Government has had two economic ministries – the Ministry of Economic Affairs and Development Planning which is responsible in planning and economic policy matters and Treasury which deals with fiscal and monetary policy, external debt management policy and also becomes involved in general economic policy. Administration of the civil service, however, is handled from the President's office.

The Plan quickly ran into implementation difficulties. As a result the Tanzania Government sought the advice of a number of outside agencies during the Plan period. In 1965 the UK Government provided a technical assistance Mission (the Ross Mission) to advise on problems of plan implementation. The report of that mission was influential, leading to revision of a number of important aspects of the Plan. In 1966 Professor Turner visited on an ILO assignment to advise on wage and employment policies. Later, in 1967 Professor R. Dumont visited and presented a report on problems of agricultural development. In 1968, Mr Schumacher visited to provide advice on industrial development.

Evaluation of the First Plan must start from a recognition of the limitations inherent in planning organization at time of plan formulation. Many of the criticisms which may be made of the Plan quickly appear somewhat Utopian when the limited nature of the basic planning capacity is recognized. The 1964 Manpower Survey identified only six people employed as professional economists and four as professional statisticians in the whole of Tanzania. When implementation problems appeared in the first year of the Plan and a critical look was taken at the First Plan document, it became evident that one necessary prerequisite was more effective planning capacity in the major economic ministries.

Thus while the Plan was an attempt at genuinely comprehensive planning in macro-economic perspective, it was neither reasonable to suppose that all projects could be identified nor that it would prove sensible to implement all these projects identified. In short, it seems unreasonable to have expected much more of the planners in 1964 than was achieved in light of the planning capacity. In a broader sense the planning performance is to be judged by:

(i) the subsequent steps to expand planning capacity, the weaknesses of which were largely exposed as a result of Plan implementation experience;

(ii) the influence the macro-targets continued to exercise on policy;

(iii) the articulation of a strategy in the Plan which allowed an empirical test of underlying thinking about development.

The First Plan was a necessary first stage on the journey towards central planning in Tanzania. It exposed the inadequacies of existing planning and implementation capacity and set in motion the steps necessary to create the necessary infra-structure.

FIRST PLAN OBJECTIVES AND PERFORMANCE

Growth Targets

The First Five-Year Plan established investment and output targets for all sectors of the economy. These targets were based upon a conception of the growth rate necessary to achieve long-term development goals. On the assumption that population was growing at roughly 2 per cent per annum it was felt that growth at 6·7 per cent per annum would be necessary in order to achieve the objective of doubling *per capita* income by 1980. Little was known about capital formation in the past, except in the most aggregate form, so that the capital formation targets were only very roughly related to the output targets.

Implicit in the capital formation targets were the assumptions that:

(*a*) Investment could be boosted rapidly with very little time lag.

(*b*) The investment programmes having been achieved, production growth would result immediately.

The current official series indicates that GDP has been growing over the period 1960/62-1967 at 4·3 per cent per annum. This includes estimates of both *marketed product* and *subsistence product*. There are a number of problems with these estimates:

(i) Growth in subsistence output and some marketed foodstuffs is derived from an estimate of population growth. This was assumed to be 2·1 per cent per annum, compared with the 2·7 per cent which is now believed to have been the case, following analysis of the results of the 1967 census. Apart from this such a method of estimating expansion in foodstuffs is undoubtedly too conservative in a period of rising *per capita* incomes.

(ii) As a result there was some underestimation of commerce and transport which are in part derived from the agricultural figures.

(iii) There has been slight underestimation of the growth in manufacturing and construction (and, therefore, rents).

(iv) Real growth in services (of which government is the largest element) is estimated on the basis of employment expansion – indicating expansion in public services of 2·2 per cent per annum and other services of 2·0 per cent per annum. In a period of fast rising minimum wages and labour force rationalization, this leads to an underestimation of the expansion in real services supplied. Direct estimation of the product (on a conservative basis) indicates that public services grew at least 4·5 per cent per annum compared to the 2·2 per cent official estimate.

These points lead to the conclusion that growth has been higher than the GDP data suggests, which is confirmed by the behaviour of a number of other indices of economic activity and by observation. Making quite cautious adjustments for (i)-(iv) above, I would make an estimate that real growth must have been at least 5·2 per cent per annum over the

Table One

Rates of Growth: Plan and Achievement

GDP sector	Plan target 1960/62–1970	Performance official series	1960/62–1967 suggested revision*
Monetary	*1960 constant prices annual growth rates*		
Agriculture	7·3	6·1	6·8
Mining	4·7	2·1	2·1
Manufacturing	14·8	10·3	11·0
Construction	12·7	7·3	8·5
Public Utilities	12·3	8·3	8·3
Commerce	8·0	6·3	7·0
Rent	8·7	5·3	6·0
Transport	7·8	7·7	8·5
Services (other than public)	9·0	2·0 ⎞	4·5
Public Services	7·9	2·2 ⎠	
Total Monetary	8·5	5·3	6·3
Subsistence	2·1	2·1	2·7
Total	6·7	4·3	5·2

* These alternative estimates are based on adjustments for the specific inadequacies mentioned in the text. Services are re-estimated as follows: Central government services are re-estimated by using certain rough estimates of output.

	% pa	Method
Education	10·5	Total school enrolment weighted by number of years of education.
Health	5·5	In-patient numbers.
Communications	3·3	Road works by type of road weighted by maintenance costs.
Law and Order	5·9	Court cases and arrests weighted by wage bills.
Other	4·0	Numbers employed.
Total Central Government	5·2	
Other Government	3·2	
All Government Services	4·5	

In the absence of any method of estimating private services output directly, this same growth rate was assumed for that sector. Note that this still allows for services to *decline* as a proportion of real monetary product at a time when it has at least been maintaining its share of total spending at current prices.

(I received help from Mr D. Johnston of the Central Statistical Bureau, Government of Tanzania, in preparing these estimates.)

year 1960/62-1967 or about 1 per cent higher than the official data suggests. (See Table One.)

There is one factor, however, which must be weighed on the other side of the scales. It has been suggested that a suitable measure of real output in a primary exporting commodity ought to include a valuation of real output deflated according to the *real import purchasing power* of the country's exports.

There has been some deterioration of the terms of trade over the Plan period; however, the significance of this shift is difficult to estimate,

Table Two

External Trade Indices*

(1960 = 100)

Index	1962	1963	1964	1965	1966	1967†
Volume:						
Exports	96	103	113	111	143	145
Imports	117	108	108	107	142	140
Value:						
Exports	93	116	128	114	144	142
Imports	105	107	116	132	170	172
Price:						
Exports	98	112	113	103	99	95
Imports	91	100	109	114	113	117
Terms of Trade‡	108	112	104	90	88	82

Source – East African Statistical Department/Central Statistical Bureau.
* Mainland only.
† Estimate.
‡ Ratio of export price to import price.

due to the unreliability of the import price index (because of the extreme heterogeneity of imports). On the export side severe fluctuations in sisal prices have had unfortunate effects, but interestingly enough, except for the sisal boom of 1963-64, export prices have been surprisingly stable, in average money terms, over the period 1960-67. The diversified crop base has tended to result in off-setting fluctuations. (See Table Two.) Making some allowances for this effect reduces the growth rate to 4·8 per cent. The conclusion, therefore, is that the real growth rate probably lies in the range 4·8-5·2 per cent per annum and *per capita* growth in the range 2·0-2·4 per cent per annum.

The macro-plan targets of the First Plan were put together fairly crudely because of the lack of real data. Comparison of performance with Plan targets reveals:

(i) The most noticeable gap between plan targets and performance is in the service sector. This must reflect some misunderstanding of statistical definitions.

(ii) Most agricultural crops have been growing faster than the targets required in the Plan. There are three notable exceptions:

(a) *Sisal:* As a result of the price decline, the output increase sought in the Plan was no longer a sensible objective; in practice, output has declined.

(b) *Groundnuts:* Output declined, in part because of substitution of other, more profitable crops.

(c) *Livestock products:* The industry has apparently stagnated.

(iii) In *construction* the rate of growth actually achieved (which was well below the Plan target figure) resulted in considerable pressure on capacity and increases in construction prices – the capacity of the construction industry proved to be one of the most serious implementation bottlenecks.

(iv) *Manufacturing* growth has been extremely high (and may well reach 12-13 per cent over the 1960/62-1970 period as the plant built in 1967-68 comes into full operation), but has not matched the somewhat exaggerated targets set in the First Plan document.

The growth in crop production for the market has been so high in recent years that it can hardly be expected that expanded attention to agriculture can raise this growth rate very much in the future. To sustain growth rates at their historical level over future plans would be a very considerable achievement. With international trade, commerce and transport all dependent on agricultural performance, and services ultimately dependent on overall growth, the upper limit on the potential growth of an economy with this structure, even with an aggressive programme of structural change and with successful Plan implementation, cannot be much above the target of 6·7 per cent set for the First Plan. The gap between the growth achieved (5 per cent) and this economic potential (6·5-7 per cent) represents the improvement that could be achieved.

The First Five-Year Plan made at least one obvious mistake. There was an absence of realism regarding the time lags involved in a development mobilization effort. Phasing of the Plan investment targets represented a smooth and not unreasonable rate of growth within the Plan period (for central government, 14·5 per cent per year – ambitious but not impossible). However, a quite unrealistic jump was expected in the first year of the Plan. Moreover projects carried over from the previous Three-Year Plan were added on to the already ambitious total for the first year. Not surprisingly the first year of the Plan resulted in a poor performance as measured against Plan targets. However, as a result of the lagged impact of implementation efforts and as a result of the administrative and political response to the poor performance of the first year of the Plan, there was a very considerable mobilization effort. (The results are indicated in Table Three.)

The record is even more impressive when it is recognized that it was achieved in a period of extreme administrative change, when other political objectives were also being pursued and when the planning mechanism was in its infancy. How far was this performance a result of the Plan? It is fair to claim the mobilization efforts in the second and third years of the Plan were at least in part in response to the overall objectives set out in the Plan and as a result of political reaction to the performance of the economy in relation to those objectives.

Certainly over the Plan period an important move was made towards achieving one of the necessary conditions for development – namely an enhanced capacity to invest. This was all the more impressive because of the degree to which this was based on local efforts rather than external resources. In relation to public sector development spending, for example, the Plan targets suggested that some 78 per cent of the budget would be externally financed; in practice over 60 per cent was forthcoming from local sources over the first four years of the Plan. (See Table Four.)

In addition to these difficulties, Tanzania also experienced interruption of aid flows from two large bilateral donors as a result of political differences. In the case of the Federal Republic of Germany this arose out of the question of relations with the German Democratic Republic. In relation to the United Kingdom, capital aid was first frozen when Tanzania broke diplomatic relations with the UK after the British failure to take effective action against Rhodesia following UDI in 1965. British capital and technical assistance was finally withdrawn in 1967, following the decision of the Tanzania Government to discontinue payment of certain financial obligations for liabilities generated by the colonial government and subsequently transferred to Tanzania as part of the price of independence. Although there were short-term costs resulting from the failure of external aid to flow in the desired quantities, these have to be balanced against the considerable benefits in the form of the heightened realism and the spirited response which generated a fast

Table Three

Gross Fixed Capital Formation
by sector (At current market prices)

Sector	1960–62 (Millions of Shillings)*	1963 (Ml. Shs.)	1964 (Ml. Shs.)	1965 (Ml. Shs.)	1966 (Ml. Shs.)	1967† (Ml. Shs.)	Growth rate 1960/2–67 percentage
Household/Enterprise:							
Building	112	118	142	155	157	173	+ 7·5
Construction	35	43	49	86	51	72	+ 12·8
Machinery and Equipment	158	166	188	275	377	400	+ 16·8
Total	305	327	379	516	585	645	+ 13·3
Public:							
Building	57	50	64	99	82	93	+ 8·5
Construction	106	96	100	110	139	198	+ 11·0
Machinery and Equipment	26	12	28	40	49	134	+ 31·4
Total	189	158	192	249	270	425	+ 14·5
Grand Total	494	485	571	765	855	1,070	+ 13·1
Monetary GDP	2,799	3,342	3,801	3,948	4,391	4,666	+ 8·9
Percentage share of gross investment in GDP at current market prices	18·0	14·5	15·0	19·4	19·5	22·9	

Source – Central Statistical Bureau.
* 20 Tanzanian shillings = £1 sterling (valid until the U.K. devaluation of Nov. 1967).
† Provisional.
Data excludes Tanzania's share in East African Airways VC-10s and the East African National Shipping Lines vessels: approximately Shs. 40 million in 1966 and Shs. 25 million in 1967.

Table Four

Financing the Public Sector Plan

July 1964-June 1967

Source	Planned scheme of finance		1964-65		1965-66		1966-67		1964-67	
	Million Shs.	%	Million Shs.	%	Million Shs.	%	Million Shs.	%	Million Shs.	%
Internal (including contribution from recurrent budget and domestic borrowing, etc.)	450	22·0	125·30	61·5	154·57	64·9	167·13	56·1	447·00	60·7
External	1,590	78·0	78·55	38·5	83·50	35·1	127·27	43·9	289·32	39·3
Total	2,040	100·0	203·85	100·0	238·07	100·0	294·40	100·0	736·32	100·0

Source – Ministry of Economic Affairs and Development Planning.

expansion in domestic resources available for public sector investment. Nor was private foreign investment a serious contributor, there being a net outflow on private account over the Plan. Investment expansion therefore represented a successful effort to mobilize domestic savings.

The differences in sectoral balance between the public sector programme implemented and the mix envisaged in the Plan had three main causes:

(i) Changes in policy as a result of new conditions (e.g. expansion in expenditure on Tanzania – Zambia communications following UDI).

(ii) Improved information about projects following Plan publication.

(iii) Variable implementation capacity from sector to sector has resulted in deviations between actual and desired spending in each year of the Plan.

Rural Transformation

The basis of economic activity in the countryside in Tanzania is predominantly small-holder agriculture, based on individual family farming units (although not necessarily on an individualistic land tenure system), with patterns of dispersed settlement, families living typically on their plots rather than in nuclear villages. One of the more substantial programmes in the First Five-Year Plan aimed to achieve rural transformation through village settlements. These village settlements were intended to change the pattern of residence, increase productivity in African agriculture and improve drastically the social environment.

This 'transformation approach' was justified on the argument that 'although long-maturing, the settlement schemes bring about a relatively abrupt transition of the people concerned to modern techniques with regard to land use, land tenure and patterns of agricultural production, and economic attitudes; they will also be relied upon in the future to relieve incipient land hunger and population pressure in certain areas'.[1] Each scheme was to involve 250 individual family farms and was to cost £150,000 per settlement. Sixty were to be started in the Plan period.

The targets set in the Plan were not achieved. In the first year of the Plan it became evident that there were limitations in both the conception and the practice of the Settlement Schemes. This led to a sharp reduction in the rate of implementation of the programme in 1966. Success was achieved in some of the schemes, but the programme as a whole suffered from a number of serious faults.

[1] p. 21 of the 'First Five-Year Plan (1964-69)', Vol. I.

(i) Expenditure on social overhead was excessive, leading to high levels of indebtedness.

(ii) Micro-planning was inadequate – in a number of cases there was no economic-technical basis for the scheme's success.

(iii) Recruitment to the schemes was, in some cases, defective, drawing for example from undesirable elements in the urban community.

The aspiration to achieve rural transformation has not, however, been abandoned but has been re-emphasized in a specifically socialist form in a commitment to *Ujamaa Vijijini*, stated in the Arusha Declaration and elaborated in subsequent statements by President Nyerere. *Ujamaa* involves the spread of voluntary, co-operative productive activities throughout the countryside. This new initiative has drawn some inspiration from a substantial and successful experiment in rural socialism, initiated by local efforts, without government sponsorship, in one of the poorer parts of southern Tanzania. This takes the form of a number of socialist rural communities run in a voluntaristic and democratic fashion, which have been created in recent years and joined together in the Ruvuma Development Association.

The high rates of growth in marketed output of agriculture (see Tables Five and Six) have resulted largely from the expansion of small-holder production. The small-holder sector consists of a number of different farming systems reflecting the diverse nature of Tanzanian ecological conditions.

Although aggregate performance in small-holder agriculture has been impressive, there are three general grounds for concern.

(i) There is the economic danger that the existing forces for growth may soon reach their limits. Certainly much growth has come at the extensive margin – e.g. through the planting of increasing acreages of cotton and cashews. Experience of agricultural growth in Uganda indicates that when such limits are reached there can be a sharp retardation in the pace of growth.

(ii) The second ground for concern has been that even with high rates of output growth, the rural sector has not generated sufficient income and employment opportunities to meet the needs of a fast-growing population. Nationally Tanzania can still claim to be a land surplus economy. In a number of areas, however, land is now extremely scarce (e.g. on the slopes of Kilimanjaro).

(iii) The third cause for concern is that rural growth has led to increasing inequality and social differentiation within the rural sector

– developments which, it is feared, in the long run would lead to rural capitalism. The co-operative dominance of agricultural marketing is seen as no necessary barrier to this.

It is, therefore, desired to create socialist productive forms in the rural sector. It is also recognized that such developments must be fundamentally voluntary – this is both a practical and philosophical necessity,

Table Five

Net Output of Private Agriculture

(At current prices)

Sector	1960-62 average	1964	1965	1966	1967*
			Million Shs.		
Crop husbandry:					
Subsistence	1,089	1,100	1,033	1,160	1,160
Small-holder	454	598	680	757	763
Estate	329	557	557	347	322
Livestock:					
Subsistence	233	271	277	311	371
Monetary	108	114	122	142	130
Forestry:					
Subsistence	30	32	33	33	34
Monetary	21	22	23	23	24
Fishing:					
Subsistence	9	10	10	11	11
Monetary	25	41	40	60	64
Total	2,298	2,745	2,592	2,844	2,879

Source – Central Statistical Bureau.
    * Provisional.

practical because the means of forcing such developments are not available, and philosophical because of the democratic commitment in Tanzanian thinking. This poses a dilemma – Tanzania wishes to undertake a rural revolution on a voluntary basis in a situation in which the forces which could make for spontaneous change are not, apparently, strong (e.g. there is no widespread need for land reform).

Structural Change

The First Five-Year Plan sought to change the structure of the Tanzanian economy away from excessive dependence upon agriculture and

Table Six

Crop Husbandry Summary

Marketed quantities

Principal cash crops	1960-62 average ('000 tons)	1964 ('000 tons)	1965 ('000 tons)	1966 ('000 tons)	1967 ('000 tons)	1970 Original Plan target ('000 tons)	Growth rate 1960/62-1967 %	Growth rate 1960/62-1970 required %
Sisal	205·6	229·9	214·2	221·5	216·6	270·0	+ 0·9	+ 3·6
Lint Cotton	34·0	52·4	66·0	77·6	69·0	81·0	+ 12·6	+ 10·3
Clean Coffee	24·0	31·3	37·6	48·7	47·7	49·0	+ 12·1	+ 9·8
Cashew nuts	45·8	72·9	73·1	81·2	85·9	85·0	+ 11·7	+ 7·4
Sugar	32·2	60·5	66·3	69·9	70·6	105·0	+ 14·0	+ 14·0
Tea	4·1	4·7	5·6	6·7	7·0	10·5	+ 9·3	+ 10·8
Tobacco	2·2	2·1	5·1	5·2	7·7	5·6	+ 23·2	+ 11·0
Pyrethrum	1·7	2·3	3·6	4·4	6·6	5·5	+ 25·4	+ 14·2
Wheat	11·5	19·1	30·1	32·8	28·2	35·0	+ 16·1	+ 13·0
Groundnuts	16·2	16·8	9·3	8·3	10·1	45·0	− 8·1	+ 12·0

agricultural exports. Within this sector the most important change in balance has come as a result of the relative decline in the position of the sisal industry. The stagnant world sisal market and the fast increase in a number of small-holder crops shifted the balance of agricultural production sharply in the direction of small-holder, as against estate, production. Nationally Tanzania has a highly diversified range of crops. There is a need for diversification, however, in certain regions which are heavily dependent on crops with poor prospects – notably coffee and sisal. The need for such diversification was not recognized in the First Plan, but has received increasing recognition as a policy objective during the Plan period.

Starting from a very low base, a high rate of industrial growth has been achieved through implementing the obvious first stage of an import substitution strategy – the 'beer, cement and cotton textile' stage. As many countries have found, as this stage is completed, difficulties arise as a result of the limited size of the domestic market and the continued dependence upon imports for sophisticated capital and consumer durable goods and industrial inputs. In the East African context, the search for and achievement of a more viable basis for the continuation of the East African Common Market may make a significant contribution to the minimization of the import substitution impasse.

An evaluation of industrial planning in Tanzania must necessarily be based upon some view of long-term industrial strategy. If the straightforward pursuit of the obvious import substitution possibilities is seen as a correct first step then Tanzania has followed the right policy; however, if it is felt that industrial planning should be concerned from the earliest possible opportunity to lay the foundations of an industrial base and that this would lead to consideration of capital goods, or export based, and/or elaborate industrial complex development, then Tanzania (along with other East African countries) has had an inadequate industrial policy.

Tanzanian Control of the Economy

One feature of Tanzanian planning was an early commitment to systematic manpower planning. The First Plan included as one of its major objectives the achievement of self-sufficiency in high level manpower by 1980, starting from a situation of extreme scarcity of trained local manpower, the result of the deplorable neglect of higher education during the colonial period. The Plan, therefore, emphasized expansion in secondary and in higher education facilities, according to a pattern which would generate the required manpower while avoiding the creation of excess capacity in such expensive facilities. At the same time a policy of restraint in the expansion of primary education was adopted.

Tanzania's first manpower survey, undertaken in 1962, revealed that over 85 per cent of all jobs in Tanzania which require a university degree were occupied by non-Africans. In a country of over ten million people, there were at that time only twelve African civil engineers, no mechanical or electrical engineers, five chemists, one forester, nine vets, eight telecommunications engineers, no geologists, etc. There were only thirty-eight Africans amongst the 600 graduate secondary school teachers.

The education expansion targets as set out in the Plan have been achieved. Eight years of independent Government have resulted in a very substantial expansion in the higher educational system. (See Table Seven.)

The adequacy of this training programme will eventually be tested in practice. The First Plan was based upon a systematic manpower survey; necessarily long-term manpower planning is subject to error if assumptions about the underlying growth of the economy prove unreliable. As most of the young Tanzanians being currently trained will replace expatriates, the pattern of existing training cannot be too far wrong; increasingly during the 1970s high level training will be producing net additions to the skilled manpower stock, so that it will need to be increasingly sensitive to the growth needs of the economy. Most commentators agree that the Tanzanian manpower planning system has been remarkably effective.[1]

Educational expansion could do little to ease the manpower scarcity during the Plan period. In a period when a high rate of economic expansion was being attempted there was also a considerable demand for manpower to replace expatriates as they left Tanzania. All the resulting needs could not be met from local manpower sources, so that the displacement of the Colonial Civil Services went along with the introduction of technical assistance programmes from diverse bilateral and multilateral sources. During the Plan period the localization of administrative services was completed but a heavy dependence remains in technical and professional services. (See Table Eight.)

The scarcity of technical personnel acted as a constraint on the level and effectiveness of development spending in a number of fields. For

[1] See G. Skorov: *Integration of Educational and Economic Planning in Tanzania* (IIEP: UNESCO, 1966).

Table Seven

Numbers in Full-time Education
(Public schools only)

Type of education	1962	1963	1964	1965	1966	1967	1968*	1969 target
A. Primary Education:								
1. Entrants to Primary Education	125,521	136,496	140,340	149,314	154,512	157,196	163,480	170,000
2. Total Enrolment Primary Education	518,663	592,104	633,678	710,200	740,991	753,114	772,645	803,500
3. Number of Teachers (All Grades)	10,273	11,100	12,044	13,576	14,809	15,271	16,580	16,900
4. Primary School Leavers (VII and VIII)	13,730	17,042	20,348	46,647	52,574	60,070	51,500	55,600
B. Secondary Education:								
1. Entrants to Secondary Education	4,810	4,972	5,302	5,942	6,377	6,635	7,000	7,000
2. Total Enrolment Secondary Schools	14,175	17,176	19,897	21,915	23,836	25,551	28,000	28,900
3. Number of Teachers (All Grades)	789	817	858	1,064	1,151	1,306	1,360	1,400
4. Output Form IV	1,950	2,839	3,630	4,558	4,723	5,004	5,800	6,400
5. School Certificate Awards	1,000	1,472	1,525	2,295	2,455	2,441	2,500	2,700
6. Form V Entrants	286	297	604	780	828	895	1,270	1,400
7. Form VI Output	199	275	463	606	768	808	890	1,265
C. Teacher Training (First Year) (All Courses)	942	985	1,180	1,145	1,359	1,292	1,260	1,260
D. Technical Education:								
1. Dar-es-Salaam College (Full-Time)	478	234	518	697	515	577	600	610
(Part-Time)	1,250	1,250	1,585	1,500	1,500	1,500	1,500	1,500
E. Higher Education:								
1. Entrants to University of East Africa	102	109	173	330	369	511	530	640
2. U.E.A. Enrolment (All Faculties)	203	305	407	642	740	1,313	1,450	1,650
3. At Universities Overseas	712	675	720	778	807	713	†	†

Source – Ministry of Education.
* Estimates

example, in the first years of the Plan the scarcity of engineers limited the expansion of the road-building programme. Also, the lack of qualified local economists (and the worldwide scarcity of economic planners with tropical experience) has placed strict limits on the expansion of micro-planning capacity.

Drawing technical assistance from diverse sources has undoubtedly brought advantages in eliminating the somewhat deadening colonial atmosphere which often persists with continuing dependence on the previous colonial power for technical assistance. It has also been of considerable political and economic value, in light of Tanzania's desire to pursue independent economic and foreign policies. On the other hand,

Table Eight

Localization of the Senior and Middle-grade Civil Service

(As at 31st December)

Citizenship of officers	1961	1962	1963	1964	1965	1966	1967
	Number						
Tanzania Citizens	1,170	1,821	2,469	3,083	3,951	4,364	4,937
Foreign Citizens	3,228	2,902	2,580	2,306	2,001	1,710	1,817
Total Officers	4,452	4,723	5,049	5,389	5,962	6,074	6,754
Localization (%)	26·1	38·5	48·9	57·2	66·3	71·8	73·1

Source – Central Establishment Division, President's Office.

there are obvious administrative problems in operating a system with staff drawn from a wide range of cultural and linguistic backgrounds, mostly working on fairly short-term contracts.

Manpower planning resulted in a significant advance towards the creation of an education system tailored to the needs of the society. During the First Plan the urgent task was to expand and to match the professional balance of the educational programme to planned manpower requirements, rather than to change the social content of the curriculum. One price of such development throughout Africa has been the expansion of a secondary and university system copied from the colonial model, which in turn had many characteristics of the British higher educational system. This system is not without its virtues, but increasingly, Tanzanians have come to question whether it is appropriate to a developing, socialist, rural society. The University College, which started with some aspirations to break away from the familiar pattern of colonial African universities (i.e. Makerere, Ibadan), was largely unsuccessful in so doing—it is residential, expensive and geographically isolated.

Educational innovation is everywhere difficult, and no doubt Tanzania was wise to choose expansion rather than change as the objective for its education system during the First Plan. However, Tanzania is now faced with the need to revolutionize its educational system at all levels if it is to achieve its stated political and social objective. Currently, the impact of manpower planning on the educational system is to be seen in the substantial shift of secondary education towards science-based courses and the strict limits placed on the expansion of the arts subjects. It is also exploring the possibilities of educational change in two directions:

(i) The transformation of the content of primary education so that the primary schools shall prepare the rural masses for the needs of rural living, rather than concentrating on the preparation of the small minority who go on to secondary education;

(ii) Using secondary school training more directly to produce required vocational skills.

A high degree of localization of the administrative service was achieved in part as a result of a system of high level manpower direction operated through a bonding system, which tied recipients of government support for post-secondary education to government service for periods of five years. Under this system high priority has been given to placing Tanzanians in government administrative posts and the teaching profession. By comparison commercial and industrial sectors have been neglected. Following nationalization of a large part of the commercial and industrial sectors, the need to channel more Tanzanians into such activities has become pressing.

Looking ahead, perhaps the most critical task for Tanzania during the coming decade is to create an effective cadre of managers and public sector entrepreneurs. Until this is done a heavy dependence on external sources in key decision-making functions, strategic for the future development of the economy, will remain. In the absence of such development, the framework provided by public ownership could very well become the setting for private foreign economic initiatives.

It is not the purpose of this paper to engage in a systematic exposition of the nature of neo-colonialism, but it is important to recognize that planning cannot be discussed in isolation from the underlying economic realities in the society being planned. While the fabric of neo-colonialism remains unaltered the attempt at planning can be little more than a bureaucratic fantasy. The area within which the local government can move is so restricted and the locus of real economic decision-making is so remote from the planning authority that the Plan of such a government is like an ambitious campaign strategy for an army of toy soldiers.

Political independence did not change the ownership patterns which formed the basic means of foreign control of the economy. Financial institutions were entirely foreign owned. Large-scale commerce and import-export trade were controlled either by international trading companies or local, non-African capitalists. A similar pattern existed in relation to control of industry, and large-scale agriculture. The reality of colonial economic control remained.

In the Tanzania case the reaction against neo-colonialism came as much from the recognition of the social inequality which was being engendered by its operation as from a full experience of the limitation it placed on development.

Social Equality

The Tanzania Government has always identified its goals as being socialist in character. This in itself is fairly typical of the governments of independent African countries – and by itself does not necessarily mean too much. It is not untypical in Africa for governments to be dedicated to socialism more in the long-term than in relation to immediate policy, and more in terms of rhetoric than practice. In the Tanzanian case it is now evident that the Government is extremely serious about its socialist objectives. It is therefore reasonable to include amongst the objectives of economic planning the achievement of social rather than individual forms of economic control and the avoidance of great and growing social inequality.

The First Five-Year Plan and the economic policy operative in the first years following independence created substantial momentum in the direction of reinforcing economic and social inequality. During the colonial period the most glaring forms of social and economic inequality were highly correlated with racial differences and reflected colonial political relationships. Within African society social differentiation was proceeding apace with the emergence of an embryonic commercial and professional middle class and the development of prosperous smallholder farming systems in some parts of the country. Nevertheless the most considerable source of social inequality derived from the hierarchy of economic and social power with the European community at the top, the Asian community in the middle and the African at the bottom. This form of inequality, although great, was inherently unstable as the political system from which it derived its support was itself under challenge.

The twin movements towards *Africanisation* of government and the economy and the pursuit of apparently neutral *growth objectives* leads to the displacement of non-citizens within the context of the same income structure, with the resulting swift creation of privileged African classes. The pursuit of increased productivity in the countryside tends to reinforce movement towards the emergence of income and wealth differentials and the appearance of privileged social classes from amongst the mass of small-holder farmers. Even some explicit attempts to reduce economic inequality have perverse results – minimum wage increases, aimed at improving the lot of the unskilled employed worker, had as their effect the restriction of employment, with a closing of the income gap amongst the employed being combined with the emergence of an increasing contrast between the economic well-being of the small minority who could gain jobs and the unemployed and self-employed majority.

The system that emerges from this development is inherently more stable, at least in the short-term, than the previous colonial system because it allows upward economic mobility, it draws support from nationalistic rhetoric and, when export conditions are favourable, generates short-term economic success. It falls short of the creation of a genuine indigenous capitalism because the industrial, financial and large-scale commercial activities remain foreign owned and controlled.

The picture outlined is familiar enough. In Tanzania events proceeded differently from neighbouring countries partly because the egalitarian commitment of the political leadership was serious enough that the glaring gap which appeared between the rhetorical commitment to socialism and the apparent emergence of capitalism was unacceptable, and partly, paradoxically enough, because of the low level of development of Tanzania. The trend towards the entrenchment of an indigenous bourgeoisie had been carried less far in Tanzania than in many other African countries; not only had the neglect of higher education made the number of available professionals very few, but also there is far less of that domination by the cultural and political values of the metropolis typical of ex-colonies with two or three generations of university education. There was more room to manœuvre. Likewise, while there are some regions of concentrated high income small-holder farming and related commercial development, much of the country is so obviously poor that the contrasts provided by emerging inequality were particularly painful, while rural opposition to political radicalism had only a limited potential base. Finally, the scarcity of resources suggested the need for a level of austerity which was inconsistent with the continuance of a colonial income structure.

The response to the growing inequality came initially in 1966 with decisions to reduce the salaries of senior public officials and to introduce a period of national service for the recipients of higher education. These measures were followed by the Arusha Declaration of February 1967.

Looking back, what is worrying about this aspect of the First Five-Year Plan is not its inherent bias towards social inequality as such – that may well be a matter of political choice, on which the technician might have no position – but rather the way in which this was *implicit* in the Plan and was not explicitly recognized at the time by planners, government or most commentators. The Tanzanian experience is not unique. Planning in the less-developed world typically involves a rhetorical commitment to socialist objectives, a technical commitment to 'neutral' policy tools, and a practical achievement of capitalist results.

THE ARUSHA DECLARATION

The Arusha Declaration was the political response to the range of problems which became apparent in the first year of the Five-Year Plan. The objectives stated in the Declaration defined the aims of the Second Five-Year Plan, while the first steps taken to implement the Declaration in 1967-68 radically changed the institutional framework for planning.

The Arusha Declaration, and the policies which flowed from it, emphasized five themes.

(i) Public control over the economy – involving public control of all financial institutions, large industrial and commercial concerns, and a major share of estate agriculture.

(ii) Development through self-reliance – involving a high degree of domestic mobilization and development geared to the utilization of local resources.

(iii) Rural development – involving recognition that the society would be predominantly rural for many decades and that self-reliance implied rural development, this theme suggested the need for changes to adapt education, investment programmes and political thought more to the needs of the rural areas.

(iv) Social equality – emphasizing the need to check growing economic inequality (based on wide income differentials and increasing private accumulation of capital) and to narrow the gap between rural and urban living standards.

(v) Rural socialism – the need to create a socialist society through the creation of voluntary, co-operative forms of production.

These principles, enunciated in the Declaration of February 1967 and in subsequent documents, were implemented through 1967 and 1968.

Implementation of the Arusha Declaration involved the complete public control of financial institutions, which entailed nationalizing the commercial banking system. In response the major banks withdrew all senior management personnel, necessitating a substantial organizational effort by the Tanzanian Government. This effort was remarkably successful – the success being made possible by the loyalty of the middle management of the banking system, the transfer of able officers from the senior levels of the civil service, the mobilization of *ad hoc* support from local institutions such as the University College, and substantial support from sympathetic Scandinavian countries.

Implementation of the Arusha Declaration also involved the nationalization of large industrial enterprises, including large scale agricultural processing; the nationalization of part of the international and wholesale trade sector; and the nationalization of 60 per cent of the sisal industry, which was almost entirely organized in large scale estates. In consequence by mid-1968 the public sector controlled a significant majority of large scale productive activity. It was estimated that 'Jointly parastatals, co-operatives, government bodies and Tanzanian small farmers account for perhaps three-quarters of monetary gross domestic product'.[1]

The move towards public control was carried out without serious disruption to the economy. The areas in which the private sector continued to play an important role were:

(i) *African small-holder farming*.

(ii) A limited range of *large scale agricultural activity* (notably tea, wheat farming and the minority of the sisal industry).

(iii) *Construction* – although there is a publicly-owned construction company and also direct construction activities by the Govern-

---

[1] *Background to the Budget 1968-1969*, p. 3.

ment and the National Housing Corporation, local private con-
structors and large scale foreign construction companies undertake a major part of construction activity.

(iv) *Transport* – road transport remains substantially private although
there is some public activity in the form of the activities of the
E.A. Railways Corporation, public Tanzanian participation in
TanZam road services, and municipal participation in bus
services.

(v) Continued private activity in *retail* and *wholesale trade* and *small
scale industry*.

(vi) The *hotel* and *tourist industry* (in which the public sector has a
significant and growing interest).

In a number of sectors public and private activities now operate side
by side. In some of these areas, further extension of public economic
activity is likely to expand more as a result of investment programmes
than of further nationalization (e.g. tourism).

The Government has a number of policy instruments with which to
influence the remaining private sector. Prices for marketed crops are
decided by the central government and implemented through the marketing boards. The primary commodity marketing system is now almost
entirely in the hands of co-operatives at the local level. The extension
service and the rural credit system provide additional policy tools in
relation to small-holder agriculture. Taxes, tariffs, exchange control and
import quota systems are available to influence private decisions in
commerce and industry.

While the range of instruments available for the implementation of
economic policy is now much more formidable than was the case five
years ago, the demands placed on the system of central planning are
also much greater. One reaction to this situation is to be awed by the
enormity of the problem compared to the obviously limited capacity
of the planning system and to suggest that the Government should opt
for a highly decentralized decision-making system with a very loose (at
most indicative) planning system. This is not practicable. Already a
large area of economic activity is subject to administrative rather than
market decisions. In a small economy extended public control inevitably
results in dominance by a relatively small number of institutions.

In practice there is no alternative to central planning in Tanzania.
The challenge now is to create a system to ensure that the economy,
now in principle under local control, operates effectively in pursuit of
the objectives the society has set itself

In a world in which the normal method of transfer of industrial know-how between rich and poor nations is in the neo-colonialist framework of private foreign investment, the problems to be faced by Tanzania and other small independent countries are tremendous.

True, it is still possible to mobilize foreign private sector know-how through 'turn-key' projects and (often expensive) partnership arrangements, but these seem expedients which make little contribution to the creation of a genuine industrial base, capable of effective growth under its own impetus. The creation of a local industrial comparative advantage sufficient to sustain an export industry seems today to be a far-fetched objective; the creation of a local capital-goods industry seems no less difficult; yet without some such development the limits of growth will be set by primary export performance. Possibly the more developed planned economies could help, by providing the means of industrialization and by agreeing to provide a market for part of the product.

Another aspect of the problem is the need to create *planning capacity*. The most obvious criticism to be made of the Tanzanian planning situation is that micro-planning capacity is not equal to the demands placed on it.

Micro-planning is necessarily local and specific. It requires an acquaintance with the local environment and some technical knowledge of the specific sector. The inadequacies of such capacity have been generally recognized for some years; the need to expand such capacity is generally accepted in the poor countries. Available solutions do not seem to be meeting the need.

One solution chosen by aid donors and recipients is the consultant. For some projects (such as road building) this is proving to be an adequate, if somewhat expensive, solution. In other situations, particularly where consultancy experience in the less developed countries is in its infancy, there are severe disadvantages. The ultimate solution is the creation of effective local planners. The new cadres will have to learn on the job, shouldering the greatly increased responsibilities resulting from the Tanzanian decision to control the economy.

Discussion of Dr Brian van Arkadie's Paper

Mr Adu, opening the discussion, commented on the spectacular achievements and successes which had characterized the educational development part of the First Tanzania Plan. The Plan had concentrated on output of skilled manpower rather than on educational innovation appropriate to a developing, socialist, rural society. This was a problem facing all African states – how to promote a strategy of educational policy as a lever for the transformation of the economy and society within the setting of whatever ideology has been accepted. The Tanzanian experiment in educational innovation would therefore be of tremendous significance to the rest of Africa.

Dr van Arkadie did not, however, in Mr Adu's view, give adequate examination of Tanzania's development planning in the setting of the East African Common Market and the East African Common Services. The period of the First Plan spanned the period of the abortive attempt at East African Federation, the rapid decline in confidence in the operation of the informal arrangements for regulating the common market, the chaos following the Kampala agreement on the harmonization of industrial policy, and the gradual erosion of confidence in the idea of co-operation in East Africa as a whole, including the operation of the common services. Also, surely, the fact that Tanzania shared in such infra-structure services as the railways, and harbours, posts and telecommunications, airways, civil aviation, meteorological services, etc., had an impact on plan formulation and performance.

Turning to other aspects of the paper, Mr Adu remarked that too much could be made of the 'control' problem when firms and financial institutions were foreign owned. One must admit limitations arising from unfavourable international reactions to policy changes but foreign ownership does not necessarily mean that policy instruments are powerless. In some ways, political reactions can be weaker if there is foreign ownership. It is occasionally useful to have significant parts of the economy foreign owned. If locally owned in the private sector, there is likely to be political embarrassment when and if a nationalization policy is adopted. The degree of external dependence, particularly the market for agricultural crops and diamonds, is more likely to be a critical factor.

While the East African Currency Board was restricted, it did have a limited fiduciary issue capability. In any case, one has the feeling that the degree of freedom of small countries to influence money supply through their central banks can be overstated.

The Arusha Declaration has been made much of in Dr van Arkadie's judgement of the First Plan. The Declaration may be made to carry too much of a load. Certainly, it *defines* the objectives of policy for social and economic change, and points towards a need for, and even a programme to transform, the institutional setting. But it seems to be going too far to suggest that the transformation has already taken place. Is it not more realistic to say that Tanzania was unhappy about what appeared to be the structure and trend of society that would emerge from the so-called 'neutral' development objectives – and that the Arusha Declaration redefined the objectives and sketched some of the steps necessary to achieve them? This question is asked in the knowledge that a first practical step has already been taken in the nationalization of the commercial banks, and other financial institutions, large industrial concerns, and estate agriculture.

In Mr Adu's view, the most important of the criteria for evaluating plan performance was the one outlined by Dr van Arkadie in the words 'if plan targets are not achieved, (nevertheless) the plan may have had considerable positive impact on performance'. Dr Eric Williams, in his paper 'The Purpose of Planning', had argued that a plan should be overly optimistic in order to ensure that the economy works at full stretch. Economist friends reported that Professor Tinbergen as far back as the 1940s had postulated the view that the plan should be optimistic, but the budget should be pessimistic in the external sector.

The implementation difficulties of the First Five-Year Plan had been discussed at some length. If one judges a plan by its implementability, it seems clear that the first plan was a 'bad' one. But the crucial question to ask surely was, did the injection of large amounts of outside expertise constitute something the plan had foreseen? Also, were the 'small international team of planners' familiar with the institutional structure which would implement the plan? Was the whole exercise an alien one that was foisted on the country with inadequate preparation?

My impression, strongly held when the Plan was launched in 1964, was, that epoch-making though it was hailed to be and was, the Plan yet failed to envisage infra-structure institutions, the administrative structure, the government machinery and the other institutions necessary for effective implementation and operation.

In effect, Dr van Arkadie criticizes the view that a prerequisite for the Five-Year Plan was that the objectives and targets should be accompanied by thoroughly planned projects. This criticism seems too strong. Surely, the first and any subsequent plan should be based squarely on such limitations. What was the purpose of macro-planning if what was said about the limitations imposed by foreign ownership of the 'modern' economy, degree of external dependence, the unsatisfactory nature of the application of the principle of judging performance against so-called 'neutral' output indicators, and plan implementation bottlenecks, while true, had not been taken into account?

On the summary conclusions in this section of the paper, it would seem that any over-ambitious plan, as the First Plan was, would have similar effects i.e., weaknesses would be exposed as a result of plan implementation. If a plan cannot be implemented, then is it wise to have it affect macro-targets? Does not the Arusha Declaration follow from a rejection of the plan strategy?

On specific points within the main paper, Mr Adu commented: —

First Plan Objectives and Performance

Output growth

It is stated that the inherent uncertainty of the 'trend' targets leads to a system too complicated for the administrative and *political* system to cope with. If this is the case, then where does the political approval come from without which planning lacks a foundation, unless these uncertainties are built into the information on which political decisions are made and knowingly made?

If the out-turn in relation to the 'potential' is as implied by the paper given the problems of sisal, groundnuts and livestock, this would be further evidence that the difficulties about foreign ownership of the 'modern' economy and lack of control are somewhat overstated.

Capital Formation

Dr van Arkadie states that the short-fall in public sector external finance resulted from, among other things, the complexities of negotiating and implementing aid agreements, etc. and the tendency of aid donors to be interested in a limited range of projects, etc. Is it not the case that the first of these factors is common in ordinary dealings in the capital market for risky undertakings? The problem of a narrow range of interests is found in any capital market and not only with regard to aid-givers. It would appear that any developing country that depends on external resources, whether private or public, for its plan necessarily has to put up with difficulties such as these.

Tanzanian Control of the Economy

Manpower

Mr Adu said he could personally testify to the impressive record of achievement of the manpower plan and programme of Tanzania. This had been systematic, progressive and largely responsible for preventing disastrous results consequent on the rapid run down of expatriate personnel in the administrative and quasi-administrative sectors of the government and the very quick turnover of personnel on short-term technical assistance assignments.

Ownership

One cannot help wondering whether even when complete nationalization has been achieved and/or indigenous ownership and control of all branches of the economy, a small state like Tanzania can escape from the impact of neo-colonialism. The control of the external economic and financial climate within which a small country must necessarily operate is so far beyond its reach that it has little alternative but to accept many limitations on its ability to plan its economic and social development.

Discussion was opened from the floor by Dr Helleiner who wondered whether Dr van Arkadie had overstated the degree of rationality involved in the planning process and required for the attainment of the changes called for by the plan. For instance, the demand for the nationalization of the banks had come from politicians not planners. Commenting on the procedure which had been followed in the production of the current plan he observed that, once again, very little local or regional participation had been involved and that the plan had been composed largely by a foreign team, the members of which were now about to leave Tanzania. What decision-making structures and manpower institutions will they be leaving behind them? He agreed, however, that there was a very high degree of political content in the plan itself and that this, in effect, went some way to mitigating the situation of planning done for a country by visiting experts who come and go.

Turning to manpower planning specifically, Dr Jolly noted that more effort had been expanded in this direction in Tanzania than in most other African countries, and some notable planning successes were to be recorded in this regard. Yet of technical weaknesses there were many and so the success of manpower planning had, therefore, been achieved despite these. Success was mainly in changing educational priorities and enrolments in university courses and in what Raymond Apthorpe refers to as 'planistration', namely the creative aspects of implementation of previously drawn-up plans for which the administrators are responsible. Of major importance for its influence on implementation is the annual report on manpower that emanates from the President's office and the decisions that are made on the basis of this. This recurrent review of policy and projections enables changes in the overall situation (of which manpower problems are only part) to be continuously taken into account – and for changes in this wider context to be made consequent on manpower analysis – e.g. with regard to wages and incomes policies. One of the most important functions of the manpower plan document taken by itself, with its 1980 target for the complete localization of staff, is as a rationality system and as a stability symbol.

Another speaker remarked that earlier comments on planning in Tanzania had praised the effect of the education for self-reliance propaganda in the rural areas but had continued to speak of the need for university graduates in economics to take charge of planning. He could see no very apparent reason why a self-help ideology should apply only to workers at the manual level and not at other levels in the educational hierarchy.

Chapter Four

THE MACHINERY OF PLANNING IN KENYA[1]

Dharam Ghai

Introduction

Planning in Kenya, as in most other ex-British colonies in Africa, has roots going back three decades or so. The first attempt was made during the Second World War. The need for increased self-reliance and intensive use of the available resources resulted in the creation of an elaborate planning machinery on an East African basis for allocation of scarce manpower, capital, land and imports. Although much of this machinery was dismantled and many of the direct controls abandoned after the war, the essential idea of planning was retained and given a new lease of life by the need to prepare programmes for the expenditure of Colonial Development and Welfare funds made available after the Second World War.

The first Ten-year Plan, published in 1946, was followed by Three-Year Plans in the mid-fifties and early sixties.[2] Although they differed in technical competence and sometimes in developmental strategy, these plans shared some basic characteristics. They were not based on any comprehensive analysis of the constraints and development potential of the economy; nor did they attempt to elaborate programmes and policies for the private sector, with the notable exception of agriculture. In essence, they were little more than an assemblage of capital projects of the various Central Government ministries. These projects reflected the priorities of government officials, often of those in the field, but they were seldom supported by detailed analysis of costs and benefits.

[1] I am indebted to Emil Rado, Ronald Silberman, Bruce Berman and Frank Holmquist, all of the Institute for Development Studies, University College, Nairobi, for discussions and assistance in the preparation of this paper. In addition, I owe a debt of gratitude to a number of government and aid agencies' officials who gave generously of their time and ideas. However, I alone am responsible for the views expressed here.
[2] The Development Programmes, 1954-57, 1957-60 and 1960-63.

A limited exercise of this nature could be adequately carried out by the 'traditional' civil service. The planning machinery consequently consisted of a few officials in the Ministry of Finance, and the Plan itself was an extension of its traditional functions – the drawing up of the annual development estimates of the Central Government. The implementation of these projects was in the hands of the operating ministries, but the Ministry of Finance did exercise some influence on it through its control of the disbursement and its insistence on the proper use of funds.

Judged by the current standards of planning, the planning mechanism operative in Kenya in the mid-fifties and early sixties can be shown to suffer from some serious defects. Nevertheless, it made an important contribution to the subsequent evolution of more sophisticated planning of the mid- and late-sixties. In the first place, these earlier essays in planning ensured the acceptance by the government of the idea of planning, and made it a regular function. Secondly, they forced the operating ministries to draw up some sort of strategy of development and hence to order their projects into priorities. Thirdly, it educated them, however crudely, in the discipline and techniques of project design. Fourthly, the actual performance of the government tended to approximate fairly closely to the planned expenditure. This was a valuable legacy to hand over to the independent governments. Finally, despite a vast technical improvement in the quality and design of the recent development plans, the core of the planning effort continues in Kenya to be centred around the capital expenditure of the Central Government. In that sense, planning today is different only in degree from its colonial predecessors.

The first post-independence plan covered the period 1964-69. It was prepared under great pressure of time, and although comprehensive in conception, it was nearer in actual practice to the more limited colonial plans. The plan was subsequently revised extensively, and a new one covering the period, 1966-70, was published in 1966. Work is now under way on the preparation of another plan covering the period 1969-1974, expected to be published later this year. This reflects the decision to have rolling plans every two or three years in preference to completely new plans at five-year intervals.

This paper attempts to describe and evaluate the planning machinery in Kenya as it existed towards the end of 1968. It is not concerned with the broader questions of development strategy, assessment of Kenya's development plans, and the performance of the economy, except in so far as they bear directly on the machinery for planning.[1]

The Present Planning Machinery

The attached chart (Figure 1) illustrates the main elements of the machinery for planning in Kenya. At the apex of the structure is the Cabinet, the supreme policy-making organ in the country. Before any plans or policies can be adopted, they must first be approved by the Cabinet. Most of the matters relating to development planning are first referred to a sub-committee of the Cabinet. This was first created in 1965, and was known as the Cabinet Development Committee. It was chaired by the Minister for Economic Planning and Development, and consisted of ten ministers from the economic and related ministries. The Committee's main tasks were defined in the Development Plan, 1966-70, as being:

(i) the review of development plans for both the public and the private sector;

(ii) the consideration of new proposals in relation to works and administrative capacity, availability of skilled manpower, sources of funds, and social benefits and costs;

(iii) the assignment of priorities among proposed projects to ensure that the nation's limited resources are used most constructively;

(iv) the review of progress in implementing approved plans; and

(v) the recommendation of modification in plans and methods for implementing plans.[2]

The Development Committee met fairly frequently and took decisions on the major targets and policies embodied in the Development Plan. It appears to have functioned quite effectively. However, in 1967 the Development Committee was replaced by another sub-committee of the Cabinet known as the Council of Economic Ministers. Its functions are essentially similar to those of its predecessor, but its membership is considerably more restricted, consisting of the Vice-President and Minister of Home Affairs as Chairman, and Ministers of Economic

[1] For a discussion of some of these questions, see Paul G. Clark, *Development Planning in East Africa* (Nairobi 1965); articles by R. H. Green and J. Heyer in the December 1966 issue of the *East African Economics Review*. See also an exchange of views between Clive Gray and Paul Clark in the *East African Economics Review*, December 1965 and June 1966; and E. Edwards, 'Development Planning in Kenya', *East African Economics Review*, December 1968.

[2] 'Development Plan, 1966-70', Republic of Kenya, p. 5.

Planning & Development, Finance, Agriculture and Commerce & Industry. However, as with the Development Committee, other ministers are brought in when matters of interest to them are under consideration. The Council of Economic Ministers has met less frequently than the Development Committee, and appears to be less active and powerful.

Figure 1. PLANNING ORGANIZATION

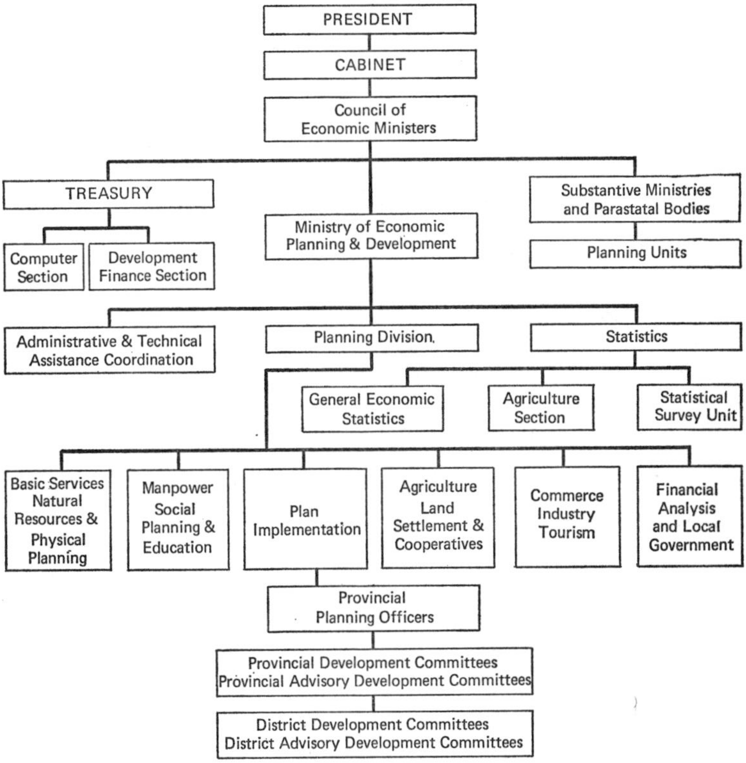

The planning activity is located in the Ministry of Economic Planning and Development (MEPD). Prior to its creation in December 1964, a year after independence, the planning functions were handled by the Directorate of Planning in the Ministry of Finance & Economic Planning. The MEPD has three divisions – Planning, Statistics and Administrative and Technical Assistance Co-ordination. The latter is principally concerned with technical assistance, liaison with Parliament and the public, co-ordination of international economic matters and co-operation with other ministries, in particular the Ministry of Finance.

The Planning Division which is responsible for the formulation of the plan is sub-divided into six units: (i) Manpower, Social Policy and Education, (ii) Agriculture, Land Settlement, and Co-operatives, (iii) Commerce, Industry and Tourism, (iv) Basic Services, Natural Resources and Physical Planning, (v) Financial Analysis and Local Government, and (vi) Plan Implementation. Each of these units is eventually to be staffed by one senior planning officer and two planning officers, making a complement of eighteen professional staff. As of late 1968, only three senior planning officers' and three planning officers' posts had been filled by local staff. The bulk of the senior professional staff is, therefore, made up of expatriate planning advisers, of whom there were twenty-one in 1968. Thus the entire planning effort is heavily dependent on expatriate personnel. The Chief Planning Officer is also the Permanent Secretary of the Ministry.

In addition to the MEPD, there is some planning capability in the operating ministries. Of these, the planning unit within the Ministry of Agriculture is by far the most important. In 1968, it had about eight technical assistance personnel and two local economists. There are also planning officers in the Ministries of Education, Housing, Tourism, Labour, Social Services and Co-operatives, and Commerce & Industry. Finally, the Development Finance Division of the Ministry of Finance must be included in the machinery for planning. It is responsible for financial aid, local finance for development, development estimates and co-ordinating UNDP/Special Fund projects. The Development Division has three principal officers, two of whom are expatriates.

Local participation is secured through a network of development and advisory development committees, created in 1966 at the district and the provincial level.[1] District Development Committees (DDCs) consist of the principal administrative and professional staff of the Central Government Ministries at the local level, such as agricultural, community development, veterinary, medical, education officers, and the chief administrative officer of the local authority. They are chaired by District Commissioners. The *District Development Advisory Committee* (DDAC) consists of prominent politicians and other leading citizens of the area, in addition to the members of the DDC. The purpose of the DDACs is to involve the leading personalities of the area in the development process.

There is another tier of Development Committees and Development

---

[1] The country is divided into seven provinces which are further sub-divided into districts.

Advisory Committees at the provincial level. The former consists of the provincial administrative and professional heads of the Central Government ministries, while the latter in addition includes the leading politicians and other eminent citizens from each province. The purpose of the PDCs and DDCs is to propose development projects for inclusion in the plan, to co-ordinate the projects initiated by different ministries and local authorities, and to review their implementation. The DDACs and PDACs, as their name implies, act in an advisory capacity to the DDCs and the PDCs.

The link between the development machinery at the local and the central level is provided by the Provincial Planning Officers (PPOs). They are appointed by the MEPD and their function is to co-ordinate the formulation and implementation of development projects at the local level. They act as general economic advisers at the provincial and district level. In addition, they serve as secretaries to the PDCs and the DDCs. They are expected to report periodically to the MEPD on the progress of development projects in their areas.

The general public is not associated in any formal way with the planning machinery. In 1964 an attempt was made to involve prominent citizens and outside specialists in the planning process through the National Social and Economic Development Advisory Council, but the experiment was not a notable success and it was abandoned subsequently. The Government has now indicated its intention of establishing a similar body in the near future. The Institute for Development Studies at the University College which has a close working relationship with the Government and more specifically with the MEPD, has assisted the planning effort in a number of ways, especially through the preparation of basic, long-term studies in several key policy areas.

Plan Formulation

The major responsibility for plan formulation rests with the Planning Division of the MEPD. The basic objectives of government policy have been laid down in a number of policy documents, the most prominent of which is the Sessional Paper on African Socialism. The Planning Division draws up the initial aggregative framework in the light of these objectives. The crucial decisions on rates of growth, the level of public and private consumption, the volume and financing of investment, appear to be taken in the first place by the planners. Guidance from the political authorities at this stage is confined to only the broadest policy objectives such as acceleration of rural development, increased emphasis on employment creation, and rapid Africanization of the economy. The sectoral plans are drawn up by the relevant operating ministries in the light of aggregative targets and within the limits of the financial ceiling laid down by the planners in the MEPD. The latter may extend some assistance to the operating ministries in the formulation of their plans through its sectoral experts. These draft sectoral plans are then considered by the planners and the proposed changes discussed with the relevant operating ministry. This provides an opportunity to review the size, composition and consistency of various sectoral plans and to agree on the required changes. The planners in the MEPD then integrate these sectoral plans into the final plan document.

In the meanwhile, the draft aggregative and sectoral plans are submitted for the consideration of the ministers. Each minister will of course approve the draft sectoral plan before it is submitted to the planners. In addition, political guidance is sought through the Council of Economic Ministers. The final document is thus meant to fully reflect the ministerial directives.

Unlike many other developing countries, Kenya does not have a system of working parties consisting of officials, businessmen, trade unionists and outside specialists involved in the formulation of the plan. The only opportunity for popular participation in plan formulation is provided by the existence of PDACS and DDACS. This is a relatively new experiment and it is too early to say how it would work out. These committees have been relatively slow to get established and start working. Local, as opposed to popular participation, is secured through the PDCS and DDCS. As we have seen, these committees consist almost entirely of the field officials of the Central Government ministries. The DDCS are charged with the drawing up of an inventory of projects in their district and setting out priorities based on some crude cost/benefit analysis. These projects are then forwarded to the PDCS, which attempt to produce an integrated project programme for the entire province. The projects are then submitted to the relevant Central Government ministries for their consideration before being passed on to the MEPD. As local participation has been sought in this systematic way for the first time in the formulation of the 1969-74 Plan, it is too early to assess its effectiveness. The difficulties experienced in the establishment of DDCS and the PDCS, the recruitment of PPOS, and the general lack of project appraisal skills, would appear to indicate that at any rate in the preparation of the current revised plan, the contribution of 'planning from below' is unlikely to be significant.

A major weakness of the earlier plans in Kenya has been their lack of locational specificity. This is being remedied to some extent in the present revised plan through the appointment of regional planning teams. Already a Canadian team has been at work drawing up an integrated regional development plan for the Coast Province. Similar exercises are planned for the Eastern and the Central Provinces with the help of the French and Norwegian teams. If these teams work closely with the DDCs and DDACs and their provincial counterparts, they would serve a most valuable function in strengthening the grass-roots institutions for development planning.

Plan Implementation

As far as the public sector is concerned, once the plan has been formulated, the responsibility for translating the broad targets into concrete projects and measures rests with the operating ministries. Since a large proportion of the public sector programme consists of various sorts of building and construction projects, the Ministry of Works plays a key role in plan implementation.

For the public sector, the annual budget is of course the principal instrument for the translation of plans into reality. The Ministry of Finance is responsible for preparing annual recurrent development esti-mates for the Central Government. The general procedure is for the ministry to invite draft development estimates from the operating ministries within the framework of an overall ceiling. The latter is obviously determined by the availability of financial resources, but an attempt is made to keep it as close as possible to the plan figures. These draft estimates form the basis of discussions between the Ministry of Finance and the relevant ministry. Although the Ministry of Finance remains responsible for formulating development estimates, there has been increasing consultation and discussion with MEPD over the years. It is at this point that the annual budget becomes the principal vehicle for giving effect to the Development Plan. In general, projects which have been included in the Plan are approved without much discussion. Any new projects are carefully scrutinized by the Ministry of Finance, often in conjunction with the MEPD, and will only be included if they are of high priority in the general strategy of development. Many of the sectoral plans are of course not sufficiently detailed and concrete; therefore, the annual development estimates are somewhat less closely related to the Plan than might appear from this account. Nevertheless, it is important to stress that inclusion in the Development Plan is an important criterion determining their inclusion in the development estimates, and close co-ordination exists between MEPD and the Ministry of Finance in the formulation of the annual budget. Disagreement on whether a particular project should be included in the development estimates is usually resolved by Cabinet decision.

Once a project has been included in the annual estimates and hence financial provision made for it, there is still the question of control over its implementation. This is provided in the main through the release of funds by the Treasury whose primary objective is to exercise a general financial check on the progress of the project. This system applies to both the domestic and foreign financed projects. The control exercised by MEPD is less formal and less effective. The individual officers in the ministry would keep a close watch on the projects on which they have worked. In addition, all the operating ministries are required to send in quarterly reports on the progress of the projects being undertaken by them. This requirement has, however, seldom been complied with. Finally, the PPOs are expected to send in quarterly evaluative reports on the progress of development activities in their province. However, the exact form and content of these reports are left largely to the discretion of PPOs. Since it is only recently that all the PPO posts have been filled, it is not possible to comment on how they have performed this aspect of their duties. In theory, the PDCs and DDCs and their advisory equivalents are also charged with overseeing the progress of development activities in their areas. As they are much closer to the scene of actual operations, they could potentially be an important instrument for assessing the progress of development projects, though their role thus far has been minimal.

The Development Plan, 1966-70, in contrast to the earlier plans, contains production and investment targets for the private sector. But often these targets are not sufficiently detailed or specific to permit an easy comparison between performance and plans. The government has at its disposal a wide range of policy instruments to influence the pattern of private economic activity. Fiscal policy, as represented, for example, by tax incentives and various kinds of protective measures against imports, has traditionally been used to induce desired changes in private economic activity, but in recent years direct controls in the form of ministerial directives and licences have been used increasingly to promote objectives of government policy.

In addition, the operating ministries can influence private activity either directly or through para-statal bodies. Direct influence can most readily be applied in ministries such as agriculture where the government has an army of extension officers in close and continuous contact with producers. Para-statals such as Development Finance Company of Kenya, Industrial and Commercial Development Corporation, Kenya National Trading Corporation, Tourist Development Corporation, National Housing Corporation, and National Construction Corporation, normally have close contacts with their counterparts in the private sector, and are therefore an important mechanism for transmitting government views to the private sector and vice versa. Most of these bodies have, however, been created to accelerate the Africanization of the the economy. The government has evolved a number of policy instruments to force the pace of Africanization in the economy, and its attitude towards the private sector has been largely dominated by this consideration. Africanization is of course an overwhelmingly important objective of public policy. But it does mean that other aspects of policy towards the private sector have tended to be somewhat neglected, and the government has not sought in any systematic way to exploit the full potential for growth in the private sector. An improved flow of information between the public and private sectors, possibly through the creation of a new body with joint membership, would undoubtedly contribute to greater coherence and certainty of government policy towards the private sector.

Evaluation of Planning Machinery

The previous sections have described the formal system of plan construction and implementation in Kenya. How has the system worked in actual practice? Any evaluation of the machinery of planning must start from the recognition that development planning as currently understood has been in operation in Kenya for no more than five years. During this short period, there has been an impressive build up of staff and planning capacity. The country has been particularly fortunate in attracting a large number of able expatriate advisors. However, while necessary in the short-run, the excessive reliance on expatriate advisors must continue to be a source of anxiety about the continuity and long-run viability of planning in Kenya.

The general political environment in a country clearly has a decisive impact on the effectiveness of planning. In a country with a dedicated political leadership united in according primacy to economic development, defective machinery is seldom a serious bar to purposeful planning and implementation. On the other hand, it is well known that no matter how sound the planning machinery, lack of political support for development can undermine the entire planning effort. The Kenyan experience is instructive in this regard.

The years immediately following independence were marked by political unity and determination to secure accelerated development through national planning. This was reflected in active political participation in plan construction, in frequent meetings of the Cabinet Development Committee, and in the power of the Ministry of Economic Planning and Development in securing government backing for programmes and policies designed to stimulate growth. Despite considerable advances in the formal machinery, the planning system has not worked nearly so effectively in the last two years or so. There has been much less political involvement in the formulation of the new development plan; consequently the officials have tended to take what are essentially political decisions around which the plan is built. Similarly, implementation has suffered through loss in centralized direction and co-ordination of various projects and policies. To a large extent, these setbacks can be traced to a weakening of the political unity, and factional bickering in the ruling party.

Given the constraint imposed by political forces, there are nevertheless a number of ways in which the planning system can be strengthened in Kenya. As in most developing countries, the planning machinery in Kenya works better on the formulation than on the implementation side. The Development Plan, 1966-70, has been widely praised for its technical competence. However, even on the formulation side, the process suffers from a number of weaknesses. Firstly, as with development plans in almost all developing countries, the Kenya Plan is weak in its 'project content'.[1] With the exception of a few sectors, especially agriculture, most of the sectoral plans are not sufficiently broken down into concrete projects. Even when the projects are listed, they are often not supported by requisite feasibility and engineering studies.

The practice of having rolling plans every two or three years would appear to have been a mistake in Kenya's circumstances. The work involved in revision of sectoral and aggregative targets tends to absorb a disproportionate amount of staff time and energy which could more profitably be spent on plan implementation and evaluation. Another weakness of the planning machinery has been the concentration of planners in the MEPD to the neglect of operating ministries. Since the latter are largely responsible for the preparation and implementation of

[1] A. Waterston, *Development Planning: Lessons of Experience*, London 1966.

sectoral plans, there is an urgent need to strengthen their planning capability.

Furthermore, it would appear that more detailed and specific guidelines from the MEPD to the operating ministries at the time of plan formulation would significantly improve the process of project selection. Greater specificity and project content could also be achieved through more systematic utilization of the expertise available outside the government. The commonest device to promote wider participation in plan making is through a network of working parties, drawing their membership from business, labour and farm leaders, and independent experts. The planning effort in Kenya would benefit considerably from the establishment of such working parties.

Lack of consultation with the partner states in the East African Community in plan formulation continues to be a grave weakness in the planning systems of all the three countries. Not only would greater consultation and co-operation at this stage result in obvious economies in skilled manpower (e.g. you would not need to make three sets of projections for the supply, demand and price of the main export commodities), but it would enhance the consistency of the three plans, in so far as they are based on varying assumptions about the markets in the neighbouring countries. The greatest contribution that co-ordination of national planning in the three countries could make to accelerated development lies of course in the integration of the separate industrial plans. There are clearly serious political and administrative obstacles to such co-operation in planning. But the potential gains from this would seem to justify a serious effort to overcome such obstacles. There already exists in the Economic Consultative and Planning Council of the East African Community a natural locus for effecting such a co-ordination of national development plans. What remains is the political will to use these facilities.

Plan Implementation

One index of a country's commitment to the plan is the extent to which plan estimates for public capital expenditure are reflected in the annual development estimates. Judged by this criterion, Kenya's commitment to the Development Plan must be rated very high, as both the composition and total amount of annual development estimates bear a reasonably close relationship to the Plan estimates. An index of the efficiency of the implementation machinery is provided by the extent to which the annual development estimates are actually carried out. Judged by this test, the Kenyan experience in recent years has been rather disappointing. From fiscal year 1964-65, the first year of the Development Plan, 1964-69, through 1966-67 the latest year for which figures are available, there continued to be persistent and substantial short falls between final approved estimates and the actual development expenditure carried out: the ratio of shortfalls to final approved estimates rose from 20 per cent in 1964-65 to nearly 25 per cent in the following two years. The capacity of the government to undertake capital expenditure did not increase significantly over this period.

Although delays in foreign aid negotiations and in budgetary appropriations must share some responsibility for this under-expenditure, lack of financial resources has not been the pervasive constraint. An analysis of the shortfall in expenditure over this period revealed that of the 60 per cent of under-expenditure which could be explained by specific reasons, nearly 30 per cent was attributable to inadequacies of administrative and executive capability, while another 22 per cent was accounted for by delays in construction and delivery of equipment, which to some extent are themselves a reflection of scarcity of managerial and technical skills.[1]

The shortfalls in expenditure in the early years of planning are quite typical in developing countries. They arise from the well-known time lags between the decision to undertake greatly increased expenditure and the creation of the necessary capability to implement it. The problem was compounded in the case of Kenya by the departure of large numbers of experienced expatriate civil servants in the years immediately preceding and following independence. Although there has been some improvement, the scarcity of skilled manpower will continue to be a critical constraint on development over the next few years.

A major weakness in Kenya on the implementation side is the lack of a well-developed system of evaluation of plan progress. We have seen that requests for quarterly reports have not in the main been complied with by the operating ministries; nor has serious thought been given to the kind of periodic reports expected from the PPOs. The Treasury exercises a general financial check on spending ministries but this is no substitute for evaluation of plan progress. What is needed is a regular mechanism for a wide-ranging probe into plan performance.

[1] E. Rado and J. Wells, 'Costs and Constraints in the Building Industry in Kenya', Discussion Paper, Institute for Development Studies, University College, Nairobi.

A crucial aspect of implementation pertains to the evolution of economic policy and day to day decisions on economic issues. New developments call for new decisions; the old policies must be reviewed in the light of changing circumstances. These must be consistent with the overall strategy of development being pursued. While such decisions and policies are largely the responsibility of the operating ministries, subject of course to the overriding authority of the Cabinet, the Ministry of Economic Planning and Development is consulted and is influential on virtually all important economic policy decisions. Basically the creation of the Ministry of Planning has planted upwards of thirty highly trained, professional economists in a strategic place in the government machinery. This provides an assurance that economic considerations – evaluation of costs and benefits, co-ordination and consistency of policy instruments with the overall objectives – will be brought to bear on the entire range of government programmes and policies. Indeed, in the end, this aspect of the influence exercised by the Ministry of Planning and Economic Development on the evolution of economic policy and on day to day economic decisions may be more important than the formal responsibilities it bears for the construction and implementation of the plan.

LATIN AMERICA

Chapter Five

STRUCTURAL CHANGES, DEVELOPMENT STRATEGIES AND THE PLANNING EXPERIENCE IN CHILE: 1938-69

Dr Edgardo Boeninger and Professor Osvaldo Sunkel[1]

Introduction

The evaluation of development plans presents considerable difficulties. When planning goes on without a plan, the judgement becomes even more elusive. Chile has practised planning over three decades, but has adopted very special planning arrangements; moreover, only once during this period was a ten-year development programme produced and officially adopted, but it was not implemented.

Faced with this rather peculiar situation, we became interested in finding an explanation for it. In order to do so, we had to go back in history and widen our approach.

The result has been, firstly, an effort to relate the changes that have occurred in the social structure of the country, including some of its political aspects, with the economic development strategies that have been adopted. In the second place, an attempt has been made to understand how these strategies have become general or partial development programmes and have in fact been implemented. Thirdly, a summary evaluation of the planning experience is presented, underlining the main socio-political and structural as well as the basic technical and administrative obstacles to planning in Chile.

[1] The authors acknowledge the time that various planning authorities devoted to discussion. We are particularly indebted to Prof. Eduardo Garcia, Deputy Director for National Planning, and Prof. Manuel Achurra, Deputy Director for Regional Planning, of ODEPLAN; and to Prof. Sergio Molina, Vice-President of the National Development Corporation and former Minister of Finance. We are also indebted to Rodolfo Amenabar who assisted us in the preparation of this paper. The responsibility of the opinions expressed in the paper are, of course, strictly our own

Planning and Earthquakes

Planning has a relatively long history in Chile; especially in the field of public works. As a global pursuit, encompassing a permanent and deliberate government policy, taking into account the interrelations between sectors and regions, differing social goals, and the limited availability of resources, planning has already been in existence in Chile for three decades.

Planning, in this modern and comprehensive sense, was initiated under the aegis of the National Development Corporation (CORFO), established in April 1939. The council of the new institution was instructed by law to 'formulate a general development (*fomento*) plan of national production with the object of raising the standard of living of the population through the utilization of the country's natural conditions, the reduction of production costs and the improvement of the international balance of payments, taking into consideration in the preparation of the plan that an adequate balance is maintained between the development of mining, agriculture, industry and commerce, and trying to satisfy the needs of the various regions of the country'.[1]

The creation of CORFO and the birth of planning in Chile are closely related to two very significant events. The first one was the devastating earthquake of January 1939; the second, the political earthquake of November 1938, which brought to power, for the first time, a coalition of centre-left wing parties – the *Frente Popular*.

The physical earthquake completely devastated the central and southern regions of the country, where most of the population and economic activity are concentrated. It particularly affected Chillán, Concepción, and other important cities, creating a situation of national emergency of unprecedented magnitude. This had to be faced by a new government, which was not only without any administrative experience, but, given the *laissez-faire* tradition of the Chilean administrative apparatus, was also powerless from an institutional point of view.

The decision was then taken to create two new institutions, one to face the consequences of the natural disaster – the Reconstruction Corporation – and another – CORFO – to face Chile's underdevelopment; particularly its lack of industrial diversification, which was one of the central aspects of the economic programme of the new government. In the political debate that followed, under the pressure of urgent circumstances

[1] Organic Law No. 6.640, article 25, item (*a*). CORFO was created by Law No. 6.334 of 29 April 1939; this law and its modifications were reformulated in the definitive Organic Law No. 6.640 of 10 January 1940.

and the resistance of most right-wing political parties and groups, the two propositions were finally approved and CORFO came into being. The Reconstruction Corporation operated until the early 1950s, when it was finally dissolved.

It is useful to remember the role play edby the great natural catastrophe in the creation of this new and very significan tinstitution and in the development of planning, which was until 1965 very closely associated with CORFO. In fact, as will be shown later, it was only in 1961 – over twenty years later – when another devastating earthquake seriously damaged the southern part of Chile's Central Valley, that the government officially adopted the ten-year national development programme that CORFO had prepared a few years before, in complying belatedly with the terms of its own organic law. Although dramatic circumstances like these facilitated the enactment of new laws and the creation of powerful institutions, they were only incidents in a long process of socio-economic and political change.

Structural Change: Development Strategies and Planning

The positive and important role played by CORFO in development planning in Chile, as well as its limitations, can only be understood in the light of the political earthquake of the *Frente Popular's* access to power in 1938. This political event, in turn, has to be seen as a consequence of profound changes in the structure of the economy and society. The process of structural transformation had started some decades before, but it was heavily shaken and strongly pushed ahead by the consequences in Chile of the World Depression of the early 1930s.[1]

Around 1930, Chilean economic life was based almost entirely on mining, which contributed nearly one-third of the national income. During the last decades of the nineteenth century the nitrate fields of the northern provinces were booming and immediately before the First World War a large and technologically advanced copper mining industry was also developed. The export sector, with all its ancillaries, brought into the Chilean economy the modern technology and forms of organization prevailing in Western Europe and the United States, and profoundly affected substantial sectors of the socio-economic structure of the country, particularly in the urban areas. But this process hardly

[1] The next paragraphs, on the socio-political and economic background of the first period of planning in Chile, are based on O. Sunkel, 'Change and Frustration in Chile', in Claudio Veliz, ed., *Obstacles to Change in Latin America*, London 1965

affected the rest of the productive and social structure, which continued operating on the basis of traditional methods of high labour intensity, low productivity, and primitive forms of organization. This was particularly evident in agriculture.

With the expansion of foreign trade the government was able to draw additional revenue and these funds found their way into public services and the building of urban infra-structural facilities. New groups of urban wage-earners and of the lower middle class came into being, joining the mining proletariat and the middle sectors which also were clustered around foreign trade activities. Industry itself developed to a certain extent, stimulated by the domestic demand which resulted from the export boom and expanded government activity, as well as by the growth of the urban middle sectors.

The changes in the social structure had important political repercussions. The development of an industrial proletariat in the mines laid the ground for the creation and rapid expansion of popular left-wing groupings, notably the socialist and communist parties. On the other hand, the expansion of the middle class and related groups served to swell the ranks of the moderately left-wing and anti-clerical Radical party. New and growing social forces were therefore diversifying the Chilean socio-political spectrum. They had their first important impact upon state policies during the 1920s, when they joined forces to secure the enactment of important social legislation.

From a political point of view, these groups and forces profited from the catastrophic effect of the world depression in Chile. The crisis produced a drastic contraction of foreign trade, and, as foreign demand for Chilean exports was severely curtailed, mining activity stopped almost completely, thus creating serious unemployment; the crisis produced a sudden, substantial decrease in foreign reserves and in government revenues. Unemployment in the export industries was followed by increasing unemployment in the cities. The political situation deteriorated rapidly.

Under such difficult economic and social conditions, the Ibañez administration was overthrown and a period of grave political instability ensued, with a succession of governments trying to cope with the local effects of the world depression. Among these, even a Socialist Republic was formed; it lasted 100 days. In brief, the worsening of the socio-economic situation strengthened the left-wing parties, but the right-wing managed to maintain control for the next presidential period, 1932-38.

Apart from contributing fundamentally to accelerating the changes in the political structure, the crisis also had important economic effects, which in time induced changes in the structure of the economy. These in turn strengthened the political position of the centre and left-wing parties in the presidential election of 1938 and also played an important role in the industrialization process, and therefore in the functions of CORFO and of planning.

As unemployment increased during the crisis and reserves declined rapidly, the political situation became explosive and the government had to take protective action. Exchange operations were placed under government control, the importation of many foreign goods was prohibited, tariffs were increased and a far-reaching devaluation took place. Also policies were adopted to reduce unemployment; gold mining was subsidized and public works expanded. The fall in income levels was steadied and internal demand was supported.

These policies isolated somewhat the internal from the international market and increased substantially the relative price of imported goods, mainly manufactures. Given such strong protection, and an expansionary fiscal and monetary policy, favourable conditions were established for the full utilization of existing industrial capacity and even for its expansion. The force of external events imposed a drastic change in industrial policy, which had its main expression in the allocation of scarce foreign exchange to the importation of capital and intermediate goods required by the expansion of the industrial sector. The result was a relatively rapid development of manufacturing activity and the strengthening of a middle class of professional and entrepreneurial groups, as well as of the industrial proletariat.

When the 1938 presidental election approached, the choice was between a return to the pre-crisis *laissez-faire* policies with the traditional coalition of conservatives and liberals, or an advance beyond the industrialization policies which external events had forced upon the reluctant liberal government of 1932-38, as proposed by the Popular Front which favoured industrialization, agrarian modernization and social policies.[1]

This was the socio-political and economic background of the first period of planning in Chile, with CORFO as both the central planning organization, in the technical sense, and also the main executive institution responsible for the implementation of the plans. The enormous

---

[1] Pedro Aguirre Cerda, who became President in 1938, had written two books – *El Problema Agrario* (Santiago 1933) and *El Problema Industrial* (Paris 1929), where the basic ideas of the government were first formulated

sum of economic power that was given to this new state agency can only be explained by the historical coincidence of fundamental changes in the economic and social structure, which brought about new and growing political forces represented by political parties embracing various shades of socialist ideology; and a growing middle class, out of which came the engineers, technicians and specialists, which together with the emerging entrepreneurial groups were committed to industrialization, the full exploitation of the natural resources of the country, and the modernization of agriculture. However, in spite of these forces, and the fact that the political coalition that represented them – the Popular Front – won the presidency by a very small margin, Congress continued to be dominated by right-wing forces which would normally have buried a project such as CORFO.

Apart from normal political manœuvring, three main reasons explain why it was possible to rally all shades of political opinion and even gain one conservative vote, which was the decisive one, to obtain a majority for the new agency. The first was obviously the psychological shock of the earthquake and the public awareness that a tremendous reconstruction effort was needed. The second was the economic shock suffered by the country as a consequence of the Great Depression, which was seen as a blow delivered by external forces on the national economy, similar but far more damaging than others like the nitrate crisis in the early twenties, the effects of the building of the Panama Canal, etc. The long history of external dependence and the maladjustments derived from the depression convinced large and significant social groups that the economic structure of the country had to be changed in order to be less dependent on external conditions. They also became convinced that the state had to play a strategic role in this deliberate reorientation of the economy. These conclusions appealed not only to parties with a socialist ideology, but also to the nationalist groups among the right-wing parties, backed – as should be remembered – by a world-wide movement of rising nationalism. The last minute backing that these groups gave to the *Frente Popular* was the third decisive factor to tilt the balance in favour of a policy of strong and comprehensive government intervention.[1]

The previous discussion explains the birth of CORFO and planning in Chile and the institutional characteristics it was to adopt. The references to the changing socio-political context also help to explain the develop-

[1] Claudio Veliz, 'Radical Conformity: Chile, 1938-1952', in A. J. P. Taylor, ed., *History of the Twentieth Century*, London 1968-69.

ment strategy that CORFO was to follow during the next two decades, in spite of the fact that it did not during that time produce a national development plan, and that it did not even create a planning department until 1950. This strategy was strongly influenced by the domestic consequences of uncontrollable external causes, hence the bias in favour of internal development. This bias was accentuated by the Second World War, which started just as CORFO was initiating its operations.[1] The international conflict illustrated once again the heavy dependence of the country on external events. In spite of the fact that financial resources were relatively plentiful as a result of the expansion of strategic mineral exports, it was very difficult to use them for the importation of machinery, equipment and other goods needed for the expansion of manufactures; the industrial and transportation capacity in the developed countries was fully taken up with the war effort.

The development strategy of the new government narrowed down to two basic orientations: social policy and industrialization. The first resulted in a policy of increased urban wages and a broad programme of social legislation in the fields of social security, health, education and housing. Its effects were impressive and lasting in the first two sectors, where new and powerful institutions were created. Education, particularly secondary and technical, was also given a new impetus.

The policies of income distribution and social legislation were, however, entirely dissociated from production policies. Whilst the former remained under the control of the respective ministries, and of certain new social security institutions which were also kept under close ministerial control, the latter were taken over by CORFO. Although formally under the Ministry of Economy, CORFO developed into such a powerful institution that it acquired a large measure of institutional autonomy.

Import Substitution and Industrial Planning without a Plan

CORFO did not have to invent industrial policy. On the contrary the effect of the Great Crash on the Chilean economy (and, for that matter, on many other economies in a similar situation) was to induce a process of industrialization stimulated by import substitution. By 1940 this process was well under way, and CORFO inherited an overall orientation,

[1] Sergio Molina, 'CORFO, treinta años al servicio de Chile', speech by the Vice-President of CORFO on its thirtieth birthday, *La Nación*, 29 April 1969, Santiago.

a built-in strategy, which it had only to rationalize and pursue in a more systematic fashion.[1]

The installations of industries manufacturing consumer goods in economies traditionally specialized in producing exportable primary products entails the importation of capital goods and intermediate products needed for the new manufactures. A rapidly expanding industrial sector results in an expanded demand for fuels, raw materials, basic metals, energy, transportation, communications, financial and commercial services. It also requires skilled workers, trained administrators and entrepreneurs. The need for urban services increases very fast; housing, schooling, water supply, electric energy and drainage systems, as well as the channels for food distribution, are under pressure. The rapid advance of the industrial sector and urbanization revealed the insufficiencies and the inflexibility of supply of these sectors and originated stresses and tensions throughout the economy. These were described by the new industrial planning agency as 'a great number of concrete problems which have been left unsolved for many years, and which require an immediate solution'.[2]

'According to its organic law, the first task of CORFO was to present a general plan for the development of production. But it was not possible to comply with this task in such a short time. Background information was lacking; no industrial or agricultural census was available; ideas about our natural resource potentialities were incomplete and disorganized; statistics were deficient. It was therefore impossible to present a general development plan in a reasonable period of time. It was then decided to prepare so-called "plans of immediate action", that is, efforts aimed at overcoming the most notorious deficiencies and gaps of the productive structure.'[3]

The most pressing needs were obviously felt with respect to strategic industrial inputs, such as steel, fuels and energy. As these intermediate products and services are used throughout the expanding industrial sector, demand climbed with unprecedented speed, and it became clear that the development of these basic industrial sectors was the main task to be undertaken by CORFO. A national electricity plan, based on the

---

[1] O. Sunkel, 'The Structural Background of Development Problems in Latin America', *Weltwirtschaftliches Archiv*, Vol. 97, No. I, Hamburg, pp. 22-63, 1966.
[2] Raul Saez, 'El problema de la planificación y la Corporación de Fomento de la Producción', Inaugural lecture of the Ninth Week of the Engineer, reprinted from *Anales del Instituto de Ingenieros de Chile*, by Editorial Universitaria, Santiago 1951, p. 11.
[3] S. Molina, *op. cit.*

utilization of hydro-electric energy, a national steel programme, and a plan for the development of petroleum resources, were the first concrete sectoral plans to be formulated, approved and implemented, each one through its own subsidiary of CORFO (Empresa Nacional de Electricidad – ENDESA, Compañía de Acero del Pacífico – CAP, Empresa Nacional de Petróleo–ENAP).

The extensive research programme undertaken by CORFO resulted in the first serious and more or less complete *Economic Geography of Chile*[1]: the Development Corporation also can claim the credit for having initiated modern economic research in the country, especially in the fields of national income and national accounts. The first result of this work was the estimate of the national income of Chile.[2] Before CORFO produced these estimates there was no possibility of having a global view of the development of the economy, and there was no possibility of formulating a coherent and balanced development plan, which would take into consideration the interrelations between various sectors and activities as well as macro-economic balances. Therefore, the planning strategy followed by CORFO during the first decade and a half was, because of both socio-political influences and the lack of statistical information, a strategy of unbalanced growth. But it achieved remarkable results in the areas where its main efforts were directed.[3]

The Unbalanced Economy: Stabilization Programme and a Plan without Planning

The global balance of the Chilean development process ran into increasing difficulties around the mid-fifties. Inflation was out of control and the economy stagnated. These two phenomena were, of

---

[1] CORFO (Fundación Pedro Aguirre Cerda), *Geografía Económica de Chile*, Texto refundido, Editorial Universitaria, Santiago 1965. (The first volumes of this work appeared in 1950.)

[2] *La Renta Nacional de Chile*, Santiago 1946.

[3] Literature on CORFO is scarce and much of it is unpublished. The most recent and comprehensive account, including unpublished figures on CORFO's expenditures and its relative importance in strategic aggregate variables is by Markos Mamalakis, 'Veinticinco años de la Corporación de Fomento de la Producción', in Keith Griffin and Eduardo García, eds., *Ensayos Sobre Planificación*, Instituto de Economía y Planificación, Universidad de Chile, Santiago 1967, p. 411. See also the following bibliography, cited by Mamalakis, *ibid.* p. 412: Herman Finer, *The Chilean Development Corporation*, Montreal 1947; Kalman Silvert, *The Chilean Development Corporation*, unpublished doctoral thesis, Tulane University, 1952; and various mimeographed memoranda and documents. See also *Panorama Económico*, Ed. Universitaria, Santiago, Nos. 101 (June 1954) and 244 (June 1969), special issues devoted to the fifteenth and thirtieth anniversaries of CORFO.

course, related, and their causes are relevant to the emphasis on short-term policies that prevailed during 1953-64, and to the new development and planning stategy that was to be adopted after 1964. In 1954 the rate of inflation in Chile exceeded 70 per cent, and the following years were devoted almost entirely to a wholesale effort to stem inflation; these were the years of the well-known 'stabilization' programme.[1]

Later came the right-wing government of President Alessandri (1958-64), which had little use for planning. But circumstances forced him, in 1960, to adhere formally to the *National Economic Development Programme 1961-70*, which had been prepared by the CORFO staff some years before, and which was hurriedly put up to date.[2] Two circumstances led to this decision: the devastating earthquake of May 1960 and the inception of the Alliance for Progress in 1961. Both events resulted in an increase of foreign aid for Chile, and in both cases the external aid agencies required that a global development plan be presented as a condition for the granting of funds. The old CORFO programme was to serve this purpose, but without much effective influence on policy, which continued throughout this decade to be dominated by short-term considerations and problems.

In 1964 a new political situation emerged with the victory of President Frei and the Christian Democratic Party. But before examining its

[1] There is a large bibliography on the 'monetarist–structuralist' controversy in Latin America: Werner Baer and Isaak Kerstenetzky, eds., *Inflation and Growth in Latin America*, Papers and Discussions of a Conference held in Rio de Janeiro in 1963, Homewood Ill., 1964; Roberto Campos, 'Two Views on Inflation in Latin America', in Albert Hirschman, ed., *Latin American Issues, Essays and Comments*, New York 1961, pp. 69 sqq.; David Felix, 'An Alternative View of the "Monetarist-Structuralist Controversy"', *ibid.* pp. 81 sqq.; Joseph Grunwald, 'The "Structuralist" School on Price Stabilization and Economic Development: The Chilean Case', *ibid.*, pp. 95 sqq.; Osvaldo Sunkel, '*La Inflación chilena: un enfoque heterodoxo,' El Trimestre Económico*, Vol. XXV, Mexico, pp. 570 sqq.; Engl. ed. 'Inflation in Chile: An Unorthodox Approach', in *International Economic Papers*, No. 10, translation prepared for the International Economic Association, ed. by Alan T. Peacock, Ralph Turvey, Wolfgang F. Stolper, Hans Liesner, London and New York 1960; Anibal Pinto, *Ni estabilidad ni desarrollo–la política del Fondo Monetario*, Santiago 1960; *idem*. 'El analisis de la inflación: "estructuralistas" y "monetaristas"', *Economía Año* XXI, Santiago 1963. No. 79; Dudley Seers, 'A Theory of Inflation and Growth in Under-Developed Economies Based on the Experience of Latin America', *Oxford Economic Papers*, N.S., Vol. XIV 1962, pp. 173 sqq.; see also his paper in *Inflation and Growth in Latin America, op. cit.;* Pierre Uri, *Une politique monétaire pour l'Amérique Latine*, avec la collaboration de Nicholas Kaldor, Richard Ruggles, Robert Triffin, Paris 1965.

[2] CORFO, *Programa nacional de desarrollo económico 1961-70*, Talleres Gráficos La Nacion, Santiago 1960.

planning experience we must go back to the serious economic ills that led to hyper-inflation and stagnation around the mid-fifties, since the diagnosis of these difficulties was the basis for the formulation of the development strategy of the new government.

It is useful to approach this examination with the import substitution model in mind, because this was the main driving force of industrialization, and through it, the basic dynamic element in the overall process of development. Induced industrialization, based on permanent foreign exchange scarcity and an expansionary government policy, meant not only a great increase in the demand for basic materials and services such as steel, petroleum and electric energy, but for all the range of industrial inputs. Urban expansion and increased incomes in the cities stimulated similarly the demand for urban services, manufactures and foodstuffs.

In order to keep some overall balance in this process and to overcome specific bottlenecks, production throughout the economy would have had to expand *pari passu* with the growth and diversification of demand, given the foreign exchange restriction. This would have meant, in turn, a highly flexible, elastic and mobile structure of production; that is, a high rate of net investment, highly qualified human resources, 'Schumpeterian' entrepreneurs and an appropriate frame of institutions, values and attitudes. The absence of these conditions is of course one of the basic characteristics of underdevelopment, and largely explains the stresses and tensions that accompany a vigorous industrialization process.

The main effort to overcome these obstacles had to be made by the public sector, which was ill-prepared to deal with such formidable tasks. The state had to participate actively in the creation and reorganization of the production facilities and overhead social capital necessary to back the private entrepreneur, and induce him to enter into and expand new lines of activity; it had to assume the responsibility for developing basic industrial activities using public enterprises as instruments; it was under heavy political pressure to improve income distribution and extend the basic social services to a rapidly urban population, it was also under pressure to absorb some of the redundant white-collar labour that did not find jobs in the private sector. All these tasks, and some more which go unmentioned, meant a formidable expansion of the public sector, both in absolute and relative terms.

In performing the new functions and expanding the old ones, the government had to use an outmoded administrative and financial apparatus. The first was responsible for much inefficiency and waste.

The second was responsible for a persistent tendency to incur large budget deficits.

A large proportion of fiscal revenue in Chile is a function of the export activities and foreign trade generally. This sector was shrinking in relation to the GDP while the public sector was expanding, and this meant a reduction of the most important tax base. Moreover, many import duties and export taxes were of the specific type, whose real incidence and value declined with price increases; on the other hand, the changing structure of imports gradually reduced the volume of imports of high-duty final consumer goods, replacing them by low-duty or even duty-free imports of raw materials and capital goods, as well as by a growing share of public sector duty-free imports. Shifting the tax burden from the external to domestic economic activity and incomes was not an easy task, since the political structure of the country prevented a thorough tax reform and the establishment of an efficient tax administration. The result was a yearly increase in rates and the successive creation of a great variety of new taxes, which resulted in a highly inelastic and inflexible tax system, if it can be called a 'system' at all.

The long-term process described above, led to an acute crisis in 1953. In this year grave difficulties in the copper market forced the abandonment of a system of multiple exchange rates which heavily subsidized 'essential' imports and a substantial devaluation took place. This, together with the simultaneous wage increases which attempted to compensate for the large increase in consumer prices, sparked off an explosive inflationary movement which threatened to get completely out of hand.[1]

Underlying this short-term problem there was a secular fiscal crisis. The growing needs of the public sector throughout the period had been financed in large measure by heavy and increasing taxation on the principal copper exporters, by means of the application of an increasingly overvalued exchange rate. Taxation became eventually so high that copper production stagnated and this tax treatment had to be revised in 1956, in order to stimulate new investments.[2] Seen in perspective, this change in a copper policy which had been applied for over twenty years, was a first step in the revision of the bias against foreign trade in the

---

[1] A detailed analysis of this crucial period can be found in United Nations, ECLA, 'Some Aspects of the Acceleration of the Inflationary Process in Chile', *Economic Bulletin of Latin America*, Vol. No. 1, January 1956.

[2] *Ibid.*, see *Annex*.

development strategy of the period. The second step – the 'chilenization' of the mines – was to be one of the main pillars of the new strategy adopted in 1964.[1]

Another difficulty that became acute in the 1950s was the lack of response of agricultural supply to the increasing demand for foodstuffs from a quickly growing urban population with higher incomes, and of agricultural raw materials to the rapidly expanding demand of the manufacturing sector. The lag of agricultural production and productivity had a decisive influence on the rate of growth of the GDP not only because agriculture still represented a large proportion of it but also because rural stagnation tended to limit industrial expansion. Moreover, it was a basic cause of inflatory pressure and tended to aggravate the balance of payments difficulties.

Chilean agriculture had been characterized for a long time by the existence of an anti-economic structure of land ownership; minifundia and latifundia prevailed. This resulted in the lack of utilization or wasteful use of land, or even in the destruction of its productive potential. It also created a situation which hindered the introduction of modern technology and the rationalization of the use of agricultural resources. It was therefore impossible to raise yields and productivity of land and labour and to obtain the flexible response of agricultural supply needed to support industrial expansion and global development.

Around 1950 CORFO did try to extend its activities into the rural sector and sponsored the development of the sugar-beet agro-industry. Since Chile was a large importer of sugar, there was clearly an import-substitution motivation, but through its secondary effects on agricultural activity, particularly on cattle-raising and milk production, it was also intended to be a factor of modernization in the rural areas. CORFO also developed a programme of agricultural mechanization. But this programme, rather than increasing yields and production, had the effect of raising productivity per man, contributing to an acceleration of the process of rural emigration.

Industrial development itself also ran into difficulties. The state had made very substantial investments in infra-structure: it had also created some basic industries. Private enterprise, heavily protected and strongly stimulated, had advanced considerably in the replacement of a large range of light consumer goods. Each new line of import substitution, as long as an existing and unsatisfied internal demand was being satisfied,

[1] Raúl Saez, *Chile y el cobre*. Reportaje de Rene Silva Espejo. Publicación de la Oficina del Departmento del Cobre. Santiago 1965.

promised substantial benefits and attracted numerous entrepreneurs. But as demand continued to grow only moderately once the gap of external supplies had been filled, over-capacity tended to emerge in one activity after another.

In order to proceed with import substitution, industry next had to enter into the production of consumer durables, machinery and equipment, and intermediate products. This presented considerably more difficulty than the earlier establishment of light industries. The financial resources needed were larger, the technological problems were more complex, the need for qualified human resources much wider, the administrative problems more complicated. Furthermore, as industrialization advanced into these activities, it became increasingly capital-intensive, and the minimum economic size of plant became larger, normally exceeding the size of the market. For this reason, or because of monopolistic market structures, which tend to develop easily in a situation like this, an increasing proportion of the industrial structure operated below capacity. The industrialization process thus reached a point of decreasing real returns.

This complex of factors, plus the effect of agricultural stagnation, had various consequences. In the first place, the pace of industrial growth tended to fall off. Secondly, CORFO had to step in to assist financially, technically, and in various other ways, the creation or expansion of industries in these new fields. In the process, it became a kind of industrial bank. In the third place, the doors had to be opened wide and a strong stimulus had to be given to private foreign investment, foreign financing, association with external capital, use of licences and patents, etc.

From the point of view of planning, the most important effect of this process was the transformation of CORFO from an institution dedicated fundamentally to the study and development of programmes intended to create basic new industrial activities, into a financial institution devoted almost exclusively to the medium and long-term financing of private or mixed enterprises. The reorientation of CORFO was so profound that years later, when the present Christian Democratic government intended to use it again as a promoter of basic new activities, it was not easy to revive its old *élan* as a *fomento* institution.

The industrial development process that Chile experienced during the last decades had serious flaws. Initiated and developed in almost absolutely protected markets of relatively small size, some of its most salient negative features are inefficiency, waste of resources, high concentration of property and heavy dependence on foreign sources of finance, technology and management. Furthermore, the increasing capital-intensive character of the industrial structure – due to the new and technologically more advanced lines of production; to the replacement of obsolete equipment in existing plants; and to the substitution of modern industry for primitive manufacture – has not resulted in the creation of a significant number of new employment opportunities.

Relatively stagnating and highly unstable foreign exchange receipts are, of course, a well-known characteristic of many underdeveloped countries, and certainly of Chile. What is less well-known is the way in which the process of import substitution has dynamised imports and aggravated the foreign exchange bottleneck. As no basic industrial complex existed, the machinery and equipment, as well as a large range of semi-manufactures and other inputs necessary for the fabrication of the final consumer article, had to be imported. Therefore, a dynamic process of industrial growth gave rise to a similar dynamic of industrial inputs. As long as foreign exchange could be saved by not importing final consumer goods, and shifted to the importation of production goods, all was well and fine. But once this process has come to an end, the continuation of industrial development requires rapidly growing industrial imports while exports are sluggish and foreign exchange cannot be shifted around any more; every dollar must be used for some essential import, and therefore additional essential imports can only be financed by displacing other essential imports.

Foreign financing is of course the short-term answer to the need to proceed with industrial development in spite of this 'exchange trap', but as industrial development has made no significant contribution to the dynamization of exports for obvious reasons – inefficiency; market sharing through subsidiaries, licences and patents; no access to markets of developed countries, etc. – foreign financing, whatever its form, soon becomes a further factor in accentuating balance of payment difficulties. New ways had to be found of increasing foreign exchange earnings quickly because the possibilities of import substitution had been exhausted. The only way to achieve this was to obtain a large expansion in copper production and gain some control of its price policy. Here, then, emerged the cornerstone of the new development strategy of the Christian Democratic government that came to power in 1964.

One final element that has to be considered is the effect that the earlier development strategy had on income distribution and 'marginality'. It appears from some statistical estimates, that income distribution improved somewhat during the 1950s, at least in the sense that the highest income groups lost some ground in favour of middle and lower middle groups. Nevertheless, the upper 10 per cent of the population still received almost 36 per cent of total income. Moreover, if the problem of surplus labour and insufficient employment opportunities for unskilled labour is taken into account, it seems quite possible that two diverging movements have been taking place within the lower income groups.

The better organized, urban, semi-skilled and skilled labour employed in modern activities has probably increased its real wages and even its relative position in the structure of incomes. On the other hand, rural labour and small-holders, small family business, petty trade and services, handicrafts and other low-income and redundant activities, as well as urban unskilled and unorganized labour and other temporarily-employed labour, may continue at a near subsistence level, or have barely increased their real income.

The proportion of the population represented by these groups has probably been increasing. Given the co-existence in all sectors of highly advanced capital-intensive and very primitive methods of production, given the fact that an ever growing share of economic activity tends to be performed using modern technology, and taking into account that the volume of employment per unit of output is much lower at the modern than at the primitive level of technology, employment opportunities do not grow much and may even decrease under certain circumstances. On the other hand, with a rapidly growing labour force, the labour surplus may well have been enlarged. One clear indication is the notorious growth of the shanty towns, slums or 'marginal' urban areas characteristic of the cities of Chile which became another problem to be solved through the use of a new development strategy.

A New Opportunity: Rise and Fall of Global Planning

The foregoing diagnosis of some of the fundamental problems of Chile's development was evolved by a group of Chilean economists during the late fifties and early sixties. One of the strongest *stimuli* for it was the controversy over stabilization policies that raged between 'structuralists' and 'monetarists'. The structural analysis of Chile's development problems, which has been outlined above, became the standard interpretation of the two main political groupings contending for power in 1964. Therefore, the programmes of the Christian Democrats and of the FRAP coalition were based practically on the same strategy, although the proposed means of implementation were different.

Moreover, both political groups had as one of the central points of their programmes the creation of a strong, effective and comprehensive planning system and were committed to use it as the basic tool of development policy.

This was partly the result of the strong influence of the above-mentioned groups of economists in both political groupings; planning bureaux were even created as part of the electoral campaigns, and entrusted with the preparation of their respective government plans; the Christian Democratic group eventually became the new official planning office. The developments reflected in part the ideological position of the main political parties, but the national consensus on development strategy and on the importance of planning was also influenced by the agreement reached in 1961 between Latin America and the new Kennedy administration: the Alliance for Progress.

This programme was partly formulated by some of the economists who later contributed to the preparation of President Frei's development policies, and it was based on a similar endorsement of structural reforms, planning and external aid. In fact, external aid became *conditioned* to the presentation of development plans, which had to include agrarian reform, social improvement programmes, tax reform, etc. International arrangements were made – the Committee of the 'nine wise men' – to evaluate plans and performance, and grant its authorization for financial assistance in accordance with the degree of fulfilment of the commitments of the Alliance. The preparation of plans and the creation of a planning system were therefore strongly stimulated, or even imposed on reluctant countries, through external financial pressure.

In spite of all this strong backing for planning, and the fact that President Frei reached office with an unprecedented popular vote and that his government was to base itself for the first time during this century on a single party, the setting up of a new and comprehensive planning machinery and the preparation of a development plan encountered serious difficulties.

One important political element, which accounts for the long delay until Law No. 16,635 of 14 July 1967 which created the national planning system was finally enacted (almost three years after President Frei took office), was the fact that opposition parties maintained a majority in the Senate. The government was therefore very cautious with the project that was sent to Congress, proposing the National Planning Office (ODEPLAN) as an advisory body to the President, without any legal enforcement power of its eventual planning directives. The Chamber of

Deputies, overwhelmingly dominated by the government party, put teeth into the project, but the Senate took them out again, adding a paragraph stating that ODEPLAN could in no way interfere with the normal and established administrative procedures and lines of authority of the administration. This was a particularly severe blow to the effectiveness of the planning system because ODEPLAN was conceived in the law as only the central nucleus of a decentralized organization, based on sectoral planning offices in ministries and public corporations, which were supposed to play a basic role in the co-ordination of the public sector. The Senate amendment practically killed this possibility.

But this was not the whole, not even the most important, difficulty. The fact that ODEPLAN was originally conceived as an *advisory* body to the President, indicates that either the President did not intend to make use of it, creating the body only as a concession to previous programmatic pledges and to the need to comply with the requisites of the Alliance for Progress, or he did intend to use it but for some reason could not do so. Our impression is that the President and the party did want to use it; one must therefore find a good explanation for the rather ineffectual role that ODEPLAN played during the last years, except for its interesting work in regional planning, in the field of basic statistical information, in the elaboration of a better accounting framework and input-output tables, and in co-ordinating foreign technical assistance.

We believe the reply to this question is closely connected with the way in which development strategies or basic policies are implemented through appropriate executive institutions. In the same way that CORFO responded to the needs of basic long-term policy lines and to the corresponding political forces, and a global planning office and a national plan were consequently – apparently – not even needed for over a decade and a half, ODEPLAN – conceived as a technical body without political authority nor even any control over the budget – has been a victim of the traditional way in which the Christian Democratic government implemented its basic policies, through semi-autonomous state corporations.

The new government's programme included the following main objectives: agrarian reform, expansion of copper exports, a strong expansion of social services (mainly housing and education), industrial development, and above all, control of inflation.[1] To carry out its agrarian reform policy it strengthened considerably two institutions, the Agrarian

[1] *ODEPLAN, Política de desarrollo nacional; directivas nacionales y regionales*, Ed. Universitaria, Santiago, April 1969.

Reform Corporation (CORA), and the Institute of Agricultural Development (INDAP).[1] To advance vigorously the government's housing programme, which was already well under way in the private sector, it created the Housing Ministry and a number of corporations to support the already existing Housing Corporation (CORVI), the Urban Improvement Corporation (CORMU), the Corporation of Housing Services (CORHABIT), etc. In the area of copper mining, the Copper Department was transformed into the Copper Corporation and the mixed mining enterprises organized. CORFO created new subsidiaries or special commissions (Comisión automotriz, Comisión electrónica, etc.) to advance industrial development and the Ministry of Education was reorganized and given a large increase in resources. The stabilization policy was put entirely in the hands of the Ministries of Finance and Economy and the Central Bank, and an informal Economic Committee – with the participation of some ministers and representatives of public entities – acted as co-ordinating agency.

As can be seen, all the main lines of the government's development and stabilization strategy were put in charge of powerful state corporations or ministries, each with a large measure of autonomy, and backed either by very strong interest groups – as the building lobby behind public works and housing – or by strong political commitments as in the case of agrarian reform and inflation. Faced with this increased fragmentation of public power and decision-making, an advisory body like ODEPLAN did not have a chance to play a decisive role.

Some co-ordination was nevertheless achieved, particularly during the first three years, mainly because this was not a coalition but a single party government, where agreement on certain basic policy decisions could be taken within the party and the government. But as this political condition deteriorated, with growing conflicts between government and party, and within the party itself, this element of co-ordination also weakened.

The situation was made even worse by the fact that the new government had pledged itself to achieve some quite extraordinary goals in the various activities mentioned above, and at the same time was absolutely determined to stop inflation in a three-year deceleration programme. As the economy was in a slump, expansionary policy coupled with severe price control achieved during a few years the near miracle of accelerating growth and reducing price increases. As copper prices

[1] The importance attached to agrarian reform and the modernization of agriculture allowed the creation of a strong sectoral planning office in the Ministry of Agriculture which has produced a massive Agricultural Development Plan.

increased considerably and the world market was very favourable, while internal taxation was also stiffly increased, a tremendous expansion of government expenditure was possible during two years, and all the main corporations and ministries set to work to achieve their own ambitious objectives. But as soon as the economy regained more normal levels of activity, inflationary pressures started to accumulate again and the planned deceleration of price increases turned into an acceleration. This was the great test, when fiscal expansion had to be scaled down and a co-ordinated curtailment of the various programmes was necessary in order to prevent a new slump or seriously imbalance the economy. This crucial moment for planning demonstrated beyond doubt that co-ordination was not possible and that each particular fragment of public power employed all its weight in order to maintain its own programme at the expense of everybody else's.

The impossibility, thus far, of organizing an effective planning system in Chile seems therefore closely linked to the way in which the state has to proceed in order to overcome its own limitations and inflexibilities. Since the administrative apparatus is outmoded and extremely rigid, each important new function or task, if the determination to carry it out really exists, needs a new administrative structure, outside the normal administrative system, in order to have sufficient autonomy to implement its objective effectively. Until now and with limited and partial goals, this kind of sectoral or activity planning, coupled directly with executive power, has been very effective. The process of development and structural change that has taken place has frequently presented the state with the need to face all sorts of new tasks, for which it was not prepared. Each time the state has created a new government entity or corporation, with sufficient autonomy and resources. This process has therefore led to a fragmentation of public power into an increasing number of strong and semi-autonomous state corporations and institutions, which it becomes increasingly more difficult to control and co-ordinate.

Once this stage has been reached, the global balance of the economy and long-term equilibrium become seriously endangered, as any attempt at co-ordination or orientation is taken by these organizations as an attempt to limit their autonomy; in such cases, they fight back in order to maintain their positions. Normally each of these institutions will demand far more resources than really needed, in order to be in a better bargaining position. As the bargaining strength between them differs, the stronger ones will always tend to prevail. The resulting allocation of resources will probably have nothing to do with their rational long-term orientation.

It is quite obvious that in this sort of a game an advisory institution like ODEPLAN can only be crushed or left aside, whatever its technical competence. But even in this last sense ODEPLAN was at a disadvantage. Although based on the rather weak team that survived in the CORFO planning office, it was in fact a new institution, without much experience, lacking adequate statistics, etc. Chile had made one plan before, but since it had not institutionalized a permanent planning system, each new effort was practically lost, since the best members of the staff always left when plans were abandoned, and even the statistical compilations tended to deteriorate seriously as nobody really needed them. It is to be hoped that this will not happen again, because during the last years ODEPLAN has made an important technical contribution to the future development of planning in Chile. Substantial work has been done in the field of economic information on current events, national accounts have been revised, an input-output matrix of the Chilean economy has been constructed, short-term annual programming has been advanced in co-ordination with the fiscal and monetary authorities, methodology has been developed for regional and sectoral planning and for checking regional-sectoral consistency. In this sense, a future attempt at global planning will certainly find itself in a better situation than the one that the present government found in 1964.

The best show of ODEPLAN has been in regional planning. Because the state administration is characteristically very highly centralized, and because state corporations proliferated, the provinces were left in the hands of the rather ineffectual traditional administration. The provinces are true orphans. The appearance of competent young staff in the regions, studying them and giving them some importance, elaborating concrete projects, helping to secure decisions on specific problems at the central level, and backed politically by the local authorities, senators and deputies, has made it possible for ODEPLAN to play an increasingly significant role at the regional level. This experience confirms the conclusions reached earlier, since it shows again that where ODEPLAN was able to find a field not already covered by some autonomous state institution, and where it was able to become instrumental for action, it was able to fulfil a positive role.

Conclusions

The preceding analysis shows the magnitude of the challenge involved in any effort to establish an organic planning process. It explains why planning offices sometimes give up and become producers of academic studies with different degrees of sophistication and of national accounts statistics; this work, though important and necessary, cannot be the principal function of a planning body.

Obviously, this paper does not try to solve the problems stated, but one can list, in a very tentative manner, some possible lines of action that may free us from the feeling of facing an impossible task.

It is clear that the basic attitude must be one of recognizing the difficulties, explaining them to the national community, trying by all means at our disposal to find the best possible solution in order to commit the whole of the community to them. Social systems in a political democracy can evolve in a planned manner only if a large enough majority deliberately consistently supports rules of behaviour based on respect for majority decisions. This is basically a problem of understanding and attitude; until it has been solved satisfactorily it is useless to design formal structures of participation and decision-making.

The first task, then, is to make the community aware of the need to accept certain 'rules of the game' if it wants to develop by means of democratic planning. If this cannot be done, the system will be inevitably cast aside by the sheer weight of events that will undertake to show its inefficacy. In this case, it will probably be replaced by some kind of regime of force.

Naturally, formal machinery must be set up alongside, so that, once the system has been accepted politically, it can channel the mass participation characteristic of our times and harmonize it with clearly defined organs of decision, lines of command and levels of responsibility. It would be worthwhile to explore such ideas as the creation of an economic and social council, with participation of workers, entrepreneurs and other social groups, as well as the establishment, as a top government organ instead of the cabinet, of a body formed both by the ministers of state and by representatives of that council. It would be equally necessary to further decentralize the action of the state, giving local governments and regional authorities the powers to take decisions on certain matters, together with the necessary financial resources.

From the technical and administrative standpoint, integrated and planned administrative reform is an essential requirement in order to make a radical change in the attitudes and motivations of public officials, to promote awareness of the needs of planning and respect for the overall policies of the government in the senior public executives and the rapid adoption of more advanced techniques in strategic areas, such as the evaluation of investment projects. Changes must be introduced in the formal structure of organization in order to eliminate duplication of functions and gaps in authority and responsibility. And the institutional network must be completed with the necessary sectoral bodies, integrated to the relevant ministry, in control of the budgetary function of the sector and placed in a position of authority close to the minister.

It is of the utmost importance that planners should have greater knowledge of and access to the realities of the present situation, both for planning purposes and for easier contact with government executive authorities through valid advice on problems requiring immediate answers. This contact will generate respect and give the planning office the greater authority that it needs in order to have a significant influence on medium-term and long-term policies. To move in this direction, the planning institutions must take the initiative in exercising the functions of co-ordination necessary for the formulation of short-term government policies, that is, they must prepare the annual operative plans.

In connection with long-term problems, planning offices should set up mixed teams of planners, sociologists, scientists, political scientists, administrators, and engineers, with the task of peering into the more distant future and giving a broad picture of the probable long-term social and productive structure; this will lead to the formulation of development plans in the light of a more coherent view of the future.

What has been written here is obviously not intended to provide an analysis of the actions needed to implement an efficient system of democratic planning, it is only meant to express our belief that the task, though difficult, is not impossible.

Discussion of Dr Edgardo Boeninger's and Professor Osvaldo Sunkel's Paper

Dr Pazos remarked that up to 1929, economic policy in Latin America was mainly rooted in the principles of *laissez faire*. But the Great Depression struck Latin American countries with terrific force and obliged governments to pursue policies of active intervention in the economy to sustain export prices, alleviate the contraction of domestic demand, stop the drainage of reserves, and promote the creation of new manufacturing industries, both to increase employment and to save exchange. Some years before the General Theory and many decades after the Report on Manufactures, Latin American countries launched themselves into a Keynesian-Hamiltonian policy of compensatory spending and industrialization that permitted their economies to survive the catastrophic market conditions for primary products in the thirties. In fact, the economies more than survived; they became stronger and grew at a relatively rapid pace. From 1935 to 1951, Latin America's gross income expanded at an annual rate of 5·1 per cent, significantly above the annual rate of 4·5 per cent attained in 1961-67. This successful policy of inward development was implemented mainly, but not entirely, through tariff protection. It was also carried out by the development corporations, which did a remarkable job of real planning, promotion, and financing. The remarks made in Professor Sunkel's paper about CORFO in Chile can be fully applied to Nacional Financiera in Mexico, to Bancos do Desenvolvimento in Brazil, to Banco de la Nación and ancillary institutes in Argentina, to Banco de la Republica through its system in Colombia, and to others besides.

The inward development policy of the thirties and forties was perhaps carried a little too far. But he had the feeling that the excessive level of protection which currently hinders the future development had its origin not so much in the policies of the thirties and forties as in the prolongation of these policies throughout the fifties, when it was already time to begin reducing excessive protection and streamlining the economies for export. But economists are always well prepared to combat the preceding depression, just as military strategies are always well prepared to fight the previous war. In saying this, he was not excluding himself from this cultural lag, because in 1958 he wrote a paper defending protection that would have been most timely in 1938 and still explicable, though no longer useful, in 1948.

Most, if not all, Latin American plans of the sixties follow the methodology recommended by the Economic Commission for Latin America in its *Introduction to the Technique of Programming*, submitted to the Rio meeting in 1953 and published in 1955. This document is remarkable for the freshness and vigour of its ideas and for the sharpness with which it shows the basic obstacles which Latin American planning has to overcome. In essence, the report unfolds a two-gaps model in which the rate of growth is accelerated by raising the investment coefficient through foreign borrowing for a limited number of years during which savings are increased at a high marginal rate. Exports continue to grow slowly, at the estimated rate of expansion of world demand for Latin American products, therefore forcing the country to make 'a herculean effort in import replacement'.

The report does not show excessive preoccupation with the feasibility of raising domestic savings to the required level, but shows great concern with the difficulties in attaining the progressive rate of import substitution that it considers necessary. It explains that imports would have to be compressed from 16·4 per cent of gross income in 1946-53 to 6·8 per cent in 1980. The report expressedly recognizes that 'the more advanced countries of Latin America have already achieved the easier substitutions' and worries about the loss of productivity that the process may entail. But in spite of its full realization of the difficulties and short-comings of the rapid and continuous compression of the import coefficient, it does not explore, even incidentally, the possibility of developing new exports. He was not saying this as a criticism of the report, since at that time he also considered exports as a completely exogenous variable. The report fully reflects Latin American thinking at the beginning of the fifties.

By the early sixties, when the programming technique began to be applied in the preparation of official plans, faith in import substitution had considerably weakened. Yet no concrete policies for export promotion had been devised. This meant that the master key to self-sustaining self-balancing development had been lost, because without import substitution or export expansion, income growth necessarily generates an ever expanding gap. Faced with this awkward challenge, planners did the best they could and strained themselves to prepare sectoral programs to enlarge transportation facilities, increase power generating capacity, improve education and health, carry ahead land colonisation schemes, modernize agriculture, and promote some import replacement industries which could be established without excessive protection. The sectoral programs were preceded by an overall growth projection that was made to balance after a few years by making relatively favourable assumptions on major exports and very favourable assumptions on minor exports. Development plans were good compendia of sensible sectoral programs, but they did not face squarely, or offer formulae to solve, the key external problem. Rather than development plans, they were multi-year investment budgets for the public sector.

In recent years, practically all Latin American countries have prepared development plans, that is, medium-term investment budgets for the public sector accompanied by elaborate projections of national accounts. Many countries have appointed a minister in charge of planning, and others have organized a planning board at cabinet level. In both cases, a small professional staff has been formed and fully assigned to planning studies. In many countries, the planning ministers or boards and their staffs are playing an important role in administrative co-ordination and economic policy making; and the professional staffs are raising the level of sophistication of policy discussions and increasing the weight given to long-term considerations. For these reasons, planning departments are working as useful government offices.

On the other hand, few governments have prepared a second plan at the end of the period covered by the first. Even governments in which firm believers in planning hold key positions, have not cared to prepare a second plan. One explanation could be that overall budgets covering a number of years for the public sector are not useful enough to deserve the effort it takes to prepare them. An alternative or complementary explanation could be that, consciously or unconsciously, governments have no enthusiasm for the preparation of projections showing a slow rate of growth or a progressivly expanding gap, or for the publication of a new set of optimistic projections which would lack credibility. He had a strong feeling that the lack of enthusiasm for the publication of unfavourable or bogus projections has been a deterrent to the preparation of new plans.

If the above interpretation of the planning experience in Latin America is correct, the crisis is not in formal planning, but in substantive development policy. This means that economists cannot pass on responsibility to sociologists and political scientists, but have to accept the challenge themselves.

Keith Griffin drew attention to a major theme running through Sunkel and Boeninger's paper and the remarks of Dr Pazos, namely that planning was in part a response to certain shocks or discontinuities (e.g. an earthquake) and at the same time it represented an attempt to create certain other discontinuities (e.g. an increase in the rate of accumulation of capital). If it was indeed true that planning was a reaction to a crisis, then one would expect the degree of government intervention in an economy to increase whenever economic performance declined. The frequently cited world-wide association between increased reliance on development planning and the falling rate of growth of national income *per capita* did not necessarily imply that causality runs from the former to the latter. We may be witnessing not a crisis in planning but rather an attempt at planning in a crisis.

Formal planning in Chile, however, was a recent phenomenon. The election of a right-wing government in 1958, a devastating earthquake in 1960 and the announcement of the Alliance for Progress in 1961 inaugurated a period of a 'plan without planning'. This period lasted from 1958 to 1964. The ten-year National Programme for Economic Development, 1961-1970, combined monetary stability and rapid long-run economic growth. The major targets of the plan were to raise the rate of growth of GNP to 5·5 per cent per annum and to increase the share of income devoted to gross investment by 8 per cent, i.e. from 10 to 18 per cent of GNP. A large part of this rise in investment was expected to be financed by capital imports. CORFO estimated that a gross capital inflow of $1,886 million would be needed over the plan period and that net foreign indebtedness would rise by $316 million.

In practice, none of the objectives was realized. The rate of growth during the period 1961-65 was only 4·0 per cent a year, i.e. lower by about a quarter than the planned rate; the rate of investment rose only slightly, if at all, to approximately 11 per cent; and the rate of inflation had been more rapid in the period since the publication of the plan than in the years immediately preceding it. The foreign debt, in contrast, increased by nearly $800 million in the first four years of the plan, rising from $1,090 million in 1961 to over $1,800 million in 1964.

After the election of Eduardo Frei in late 1964 on a programme of 'revolution in liberty' a new phase began. In the field of formal planning Frei's revolution eventually led to the creation of ODEPLAN. The best qualified economists at ODEPLAN, however, both before and after its legal establishment, were concerned with global programming, the

construction of an input-output table and the preparation of a simula-
tion model of the economy. These activities were only tenuously related
to the government's development policies. Indeed, while the planners
were playing with macro-models, the rest of the government was trying
to implement a series of sectoral policies.

One of the obstacles to good planning was the absence of statistics.
Professor Sunkel said that planning efforts throughout Latin America
had been cyclical. Bursts of energy had been devoted to gathering
statistics on a once-and-for-all basis to produce a plan, while relatively
little effort has been devoted to organizing an adequate statistical
system. Why had a sustained effort to improve the quantity and quality
of data been lacking? Why had it been impossible to organize a decent
statistical service? The reasons were unclear. In general, however, economists had paid little attention to statistics; they used but did not
produce them, and little prestige was attached to working as a statistician.

It had been suggested that in view of the numerous obstacles to
comprehensive planning in Chile it might be possible to push ahead in
certain key areas even if other sectors lagged behind. Chile, for example,
was said to have solved – or nearly solved – its export problem and the
question of the ownership of its copper wealth; it had introduced a
system of frequent but small devaluations which had neutralized the
effect of inflation on the balance of payments. Improvements had been
made in education and the agrarian reform is moving ahead. Some
advances might be possible even if these occurred in an unbalanced way.

While unbalanced growth of this type clearly was possible, it would
be wrong (Griffin argued) to exaggerate the achievements in Chile. For
instance, the targets for agrarian reform had been reduced repeatedly
from the original objective of settling 100,000 families in six years to a
current target of 40,000. As of May 1968 only 9,050 families had been
settled in *asentamientos* and there was yet to be prepared an accurate
assessment of the benefits and costs of this programme. By the end of
Frei's term of office perhaps 25-30,000 families would have benefited
from land reform. This would represent an achievement of less than
a third of the original objective.

The way in which copper policy was formulated also was distressing.
Seven weeks after coming to power Frei announced the partial nationalization of the copper industry and an expansion programme that would
cost over half a billion dollars. Only a rudimentary effort was made to
assess the benefits and costs of this copper policy to Chile, and it
subsequently emerged that the net benefits were negligible, particularly

the net benefits of the 51 per cent nationalization of the Braden Co. One now read in the financial press, four and a half years after the copper policy was announced, that the government was dissatisfied with the agreement reached with the foreign corporations and had reopened negotiations with the intention of raising taxation and increasing Chilean ownership of the mines. Surely it would have been better if, several years ago, the planners had devoted more attention to copper policy and less attention to macro-economic models. Surely the largest single project in the country deserved closer economic scrutiny than could be provided by an engineer and an accountant in seven weeks.

Continuing the discussion, Dudley Seers doubted whether Sunkel had paid enough attention to the weakness of statistics. For example, at least until recently, official national income series had been obtained by deflating current-value series by a consumer price index, the weighting of which had been derived from a survey of working-class households (in Santiago only) before the last war. As revisions indicated, the results had little value. In many 'developing' countries, one could not really reach any conclusions on the rate of increase in the national income from published statistics. In such circumstances, planning was very difficult; quantitative projections of any sophistication were quite meaningless. Moreover, the case for omitting non-economic elements from planning on the grounds that they are not quantifiable, is greatly weakened if economic factors cannot really be quantified either.

Chile presented a puzzle. There were plenty of very able analysts of its experiences and prospects; there was no general shortage of professionally qualified people in the administration or the private sector – indeed the country exported economists; and one could not really talk of a lack of political will. Despite what Boeninger had said, there was considerable agreement on the reforms needed, by international standards. Why was development so slow?

There was a chronic lack of co-ordination inside government. Ministries were unwilling to give up their autonomy. This raised questions in the first place about the training of civil servants and – more basically – about the educational system as a whole; and second, about the cumbersome congressional system and its traditions of passing laws which reinforced bureaucracy.

These in turn posed issues about the questions of the role of the individual – a question which social scientists, unlike journalists, tend to underplay because of the disruptive effect it has on their theories. Could somebody else other than Eduardo Frei have changed the basic constraints on development? Would these have been more successfully modified if Jorge Ahumada had lived?

Finally, how much was financial aid obstructing development? Chile is rich in natural and human resources; was aid postponing the day on which aid would no longer be needed, by making it possible to avoid awkward decisions? However necessary aid was to some countries, in a case like Chile it might be obstructing development by removing the urgency from (e.g.) fiscal reforms, by superimposing the priorities of aid agencies on policy, (through 'performance criteria' and other conditions), and by undermining the feeling of self-reliance.

There was a theme, albeit a fairly muted one, to the rest of the discussion: that of the immense importance of structural factors, and the necessity for planning both to reflect it, and to induce structural change. Far less muted was Dr Griffin's reiterated charge of pseudo-planning levelled at Latin American countries on the grounds that plans were irrelevant to policy formation and, in some cases, difficult or impossible to find. It was further argued that the coincidence of the formation of the Alliance for Progress with the rise in planning in Latin America was significant, as was the initial emphasis on structural reforms in the wake of the Cuban revolution. By the second Punta del Este, attention had shifted away from structural reforms and towards LAFTA. Yet the crisis in development policy stemmed from unchanging institutions and structures.

The controversy over the merits of institutional as opposed to a technical approach to planning was taken up by Professor Sunkel in his reply. He saw the distinction between them as incorrect. Anyone could produce a macro-dynamic model, but few a relevant one fusing together both technical and institutional elements. Ecuador, for example, needed a two-country or two-region model, while actual experience in Chile provided a case in point. A recent plan had been based on an assumption of a large expansion of the copper industry, yet there was no model to analyse the attendant effects of such a development. Statistical procedures also came under fire. Frantic efforts were made to collect data during the period of plan formulation, but the on-going work of collection was often neglected. Moreover, the data which was gathered was useful for UN purposes, but inappropriate for planning in Chile.

As regards the role of foreign aid and technical assistance, Professor Sunkel agreed with Dudley Seers. In certain countries aid was essential, but in Chile it was not. In fact, foreign aid had two bad effects. First, it enabled the government to take (or not take) decisions without having to assume full responsibility for the consequences of its decisions. Second, aid tended to increase the supply of dedicated foreign experts who are well trained in macro-economics but who knew little of institutional economics, usually had had no administrative experience and who knew nothing of Chile's aims and possibilities. The contribution of such people on the margin often was negative.

Why had planning failed? Professor Boeninger thought there were a few technical reasons. First, there was no adequate network for sectoral planning. On this point he disagreed with Professor Sunkel. The semi-autonomous public corporations made economic decisions but could not be said to plan. Second, the public administration was overburdened with work and had been unable to add the tasks of planning to its traditional activities. Finally, the work of ODEPLAN had not been timely: its reports had been completed too late to influence policy and as a result it had little authority and commanded little respect. In reply to Dudley Seers' observation, Professor Boeninger said that he did not believe that Ahumada could have overcome the obstacles to planning if he had lived. Ahumada worked as chief planner for a year before he died, and was beginning to encounter these difficulties. The basic reasons for the failure of planning lay elsewhere, however. There was, above all, the pronounced ideological conflict over whether the nation was to be capitalist, socialist or whatever. This meant that policies inevitably were based on a series of compromises among political groups, and as a result were bound to be inconsistent and contradictory.

Concluding the discussion, Dr Pazos was both energetic and charming. He reiterated his position that the substantive policy problems must be solved and then incorporated in the planning mechanism. He also took strong exception to the view that planning began in Latin America with the first Punta del Este. In fact, the movement towards planning began in ECLA in the early fifties despite opposition from the monetarist school in the US. Two plans had been formulated and approved before the Alliance for Progress and a second wave of plans had also been prepared. Lastly, there was no question that both political scientists and sociologists did have roles to play in the planning process – but economists still had to solve the problems which fell within their province without making appeals elsewhere.

Planning the Improvement of Planning in Latin America, *by* Sra I. de Navarrete and K. B. Griffin

The Context

Most of Latin America is in constant political turmoil. The first of the great revolutions of this century occurred in Mexico. This was followed in 1952 by the Bolivian revolution and in 1959 by the Cuban revolution. Surrounding these major social upheavals have been a series of revolts, rebellions, urban riots, guerrilla movements, palace coups. The violence and instability of the region is caused by, and is a reflection of, a sharp inequality in the distribution of income and wealth, sharp social differentiation and sometimes repressive political institutions. These basic considerations must be taken into account when the possibilities, purposes, and scope of planning are considered. Moreover, the political instability of the region can be expected to continue. Planning in this context must necessarily be concerned with introducing structural and institutional changes, upon which social peace and economic development depend.

The Latin American Republics vary in size and stage of development. The big six (Brazil, Colombia, Argentina, Chile, Venezuela, and Mexico) have a population close to 200 million people. Furthermore, in most countries of the region the population is increasing by 2·5-3·5 per cent a year, although the rate of increase in Argentina and Uruguay is much lower. The level of annual *per capita* income varies from roughly 140 dollars to over 700, and there are equally wide variations within each country.

Income distribution is highly unequal. In some countries inequality seems to be increasing although *per capita* income of the poorest group is also rising, even if very slowly. In others, e.g. Argentina, increased income inequality and a slow growth of output have combined in the last decade or so to lower the standard of living of large segments of the population in absolute terms. In still other countries inequality is most apparent in the form of large and increasing differences in the regional distribution of income. Northeast Brazil, and the Peruvian Sierra are examples of this. Finally, in at least one country, Uruguay, in which there was a lesser inequality in the distribution of income, aggregate *per capita* income has been declining for over ten years. In Chile, in contrast to most of Latin America, the distribution of income has recently improved.

In general a small proportion of the population (5-10 per cent) receives a large part of the national income (30-50 per cent). This concentration of purchasing power reduces the size of the domestic market and tends to lead to a waste of resources in conspicuous consumption. Furthermore, the export of capital by the rich and their demand for imported consumer durables exacerbates foreign exchange difficulties. Finally the unequal distribution of income leads to a pattern of investment which is not always the most productive from the social point of view.

With few exceptions the tax system favours concentration of income and wealth although some progress has been made recently in reducing the regressiveness of taxation and increasing the ratio of taxes to national income, especially in Chile. The tax/GDP ratio varies from one country to another, being unusually low in Mexico and Paraguay and considerably higher in Brazil, Chile and Argentina. The growth of the public sector and the provision of collective consumption could help to redress income inequalities, but this has not as yet acted as a strong corrective mechanism in most countries.

All the Latin American countries are open economies and the foreign trade sector is very important. The reason for the importance of foreign trade lies not in the relative size of the sector, which differs from one country to another, but in the fact that the export sector fulfils the role of the capital and intermediate goods industries. For this reason the stability and rate of growth of the economy as a whole depends to a considerable degree upon the stability and rate of growth of foreign exchange earnings. Unfortunately exports – and particularly the more traditional exports – have failed to grow rapidly in the last two decades. In part this is due to bad policies within Latin America which have not provided incentives for diversifying exports. On the other hand, there have also been a series of external factors which have reduced the rate of growth of foreign exchange earnings: low income elasticities of demand for tropical products such as coffee and sugar; technical substitution of synthetic materials such as plastic for some of the metals; the establishment of preferential trading agreements between some European countries and their former African colonies; and investment by some of the large international corporations in the low tax, low wage, mineral abundant countries of Central Africa and the Middle East rather than in Latin America where profit rates are lower.

While export earnings have grown slowly the demand for imports has increased rapidly, and the tendency for the balance of payments to get into deficit has been overcome in the short-run by swiftly rising foreign indebtedness. Thus the heavy dependence on foreign loans and investment is due in part to the failure of exports to grow fast enough to finance desired imports. At the same time, it could be argued that the availability of foreign capital has reduced the pressure to seek ways of promoting exports. It is generally agreed that one of the objectives of planning should be to reduce the dependence on aid and, where possible, improve the use to which existing foreign exchange earnings are put.

One way in which the Latin American countries have tried to cope with the balance of payments problem is by import substituting industrialization. The strategy of *desarrollo hacia adentro* has been biased in favour of the urban areas in general and the consumer goods industries in particular. In few areas, until quite recently, has attention been devoted to improving conditions in rural zones or in developing capital goods industries. As a result of the strategy pursued, the structure of the economically active population is that of an agricultural economy in transition to an industrial one. The labour force in agriculture varies from 30 per cent in Argentina to 65 per cent in Venezuela, and an even higher proportion in Paraguay, Bolivia and Ecuador. However, the value of production generated in agriculture is much lower and reflects the inefficient and inequitable land tenure system that prevails throughout much of the region. Indeed the poor performance of agriculture together with the fact that a large fraction of the labour force is still engaged in this sector is one of the main structural problems that must be overcome.

The need for an agrarian reform has been discussed for many years, but apart from Bolivia, Cuba and Mexico almost nothing has been done until very recently. In fact, even in Mexico it has been argued that the land reform did not go far enough to solve the problem of distributive justice although the problems of production were overcome, notably on medium and large commercial farms. In the last few years some progress has been made in Chile, Venezuela and Colombia, and Peru has just announced its intention to implement a radical reform. However, it has not been possible to provide enough economic opportunities in rural areas to prevent massive internal migrations to the cities and rapid urbanization. The concentration of social services in the cities, particularly education and health facilities, has merely accentuated the trend.

Rapid urbanization has not led to acute urban unemployment except in some Caribbean islands. In most countries the potential unemployment has been absorbed into the public administration and petty services where it has become, in effect, disguised unemployment. The creation of productive employment opportunities in both the rural and urban areas has become a serious problem. It is unlikely that industry will grow sufficiently rapidly to provide employment for those entering the labour force. A possibility exists, however, of creating additional employment in some of the basic services, e.g. in educational and public health activities. In the longer run a reduction in the rate of population growth may help to alleviate problems of underemployment.

Latin America is well provided with professional manpower in comparison with most underdeveloped regions. Skilled labour and qualified technicians, however, are scarce. In some countries, particularly Colombia, Argentina and the Central American nations, a 'skill drain' of doctors, nurses and engineers to the United States has become quite serious. Moreover, the problem is likely to become worse since the stock of professional manpower is growing more rapidly than the economy. Already it is probable that Latin America is a net contributor of technical assistance to the United States.

The loss of human capital to the industrial nations has created difficulties, but these have been slight in comparison with the problems created by the presence of large amounts of direct private foreign investment in the region. Foreign investment in the past has been concentrated in the mineral extractive industries and plantation crops. More recently, however, the pattern has changed and increasing amounts of foreign investment are occurring in manufacturing activities. One reason for the shift in interest is the tendency for extractive industries to be nationalized, e.g. petroleum in Mexico and Peru, tin in Bolivia and copper in Chile. Another is the increase in the size of the domestic market as a consequence of industrialization and growth. The increasing preoccupation in Argentina, Brazil and Mexico with the penetration of foreign capital into their industrial sectors is indicative of the need for an official policy in this sphere. It is believed by many that foreign firms are purchasing existing local enterprises rather than creating new ones and that this has the effect of converting local entrepreneurs into rentiers. Others fear that the subsidiaries of large international firms will be reluctant to export manufactured goods in competition with the parent firm. Still others worry whether foreign private capital can be associated with national objectives and integrated with development planning. Mixed public and foreign private enterprises are sometimes suggested as a solution.

The private sector, of course, is important in all the countries we are discussing. Agriculture, most light and heavy industry, and many service activities are in private hands, and the presence of this large private sector constitutes a special problem for planning.

A further problem arises from the fact that the quality of the public administration is not homogeneous. Some Ministries, especially the technical ones and those that deal with public works, often are quick and efficient, but others are slow, inefficient and plagued by corruption. In general, the large number of semi-autonomous public corporations have functioned somewhat better than the traditional public administration, but the fragmentation of authority which these institutions create accentuates some problems of planning.

There are many weaknesses in planning as it is currently practised in Latin America. Plan formulation is separate from the provision for implementation. In Mexico a six-year plan was drawn as early as 1934 but it was not followed by the creation of a planning mechanism until 1954. The plans themselves often are excessively elaborate and time-consuming; at the same time, they lack a central strategy for development. In practice, policy usually is concerned with overcoming short-run difficulties and the long-run is neglected: the 'urgent' takes priority over the merely 'important'. Important interests are poorly represented in the planning process, particularly (a) future generations and (b) large groups in the community who are unorganized and lack political power. Indeed, in many cases groups either are prevented from becoming organized (e.g. laws which make agricultural labour unions illegal) or are repressed if they do become organized (e.g. the peasant leagues in Brazil).

There has been only one attempt in Latin America at planned international co-operation – the Alliance for Progress. It is generally recognized that this has failed in achieving its objectives of combining rapid growth with structural reforms within the framework of multilateral co-operation. There have also been two major attempts at regional co-operation and co-ordination of development – the Central American Common Market and the Latin American Free Trade Association. So far neither of these organizations has had much relevance for planning. However, LAFTA and other regional organizations like ECLA and CECLA have served as a forum for debating questions of common interest and a consensus has been formed as to the demands of Latin America (and the other developing countries in UNCTAD) *vis-à-vis* the developed nations.

In practice it seems the purpose of planning has been in part to obtain foreign assistance under the Alliance for Progress; in part to maintain and strengthen the *status quo*, i.e. to avoid the necessity of structural reforms; and in part it has been an heroic attempt by a few technocrats and United Nations officials to introduce rational economic management into the public sector. For all these reasons Latin America has largely engaged in 'pseudo planning' and in some instances the very idea of planning is in danger of becoming discredited.

EUROPE

Chapter Six

DEVELOPMENT AND CHANGES IN CONCEPTIONS OF PLANNING IN SOCIALIST COUNTRIES

Professor Arnost Tauber

Any social system, and in consequence even a socialist society, preserves in general its political character. Neither in the theoretical nor in the practical field, in particular in economics, can one neglect this fact. In the course of the development of the socialist society there may be stages when politics must be in any case given priority; probably later on, it will reach a stage where economics will be determinant. However, always there is a very close interconnection between politics and economics.

Without a preponderance of politics in the reciprocal relations between politics and economics, the transformation of a capitalist society, with its essential characteristic of private ownership, to a socialist society characterized mainly by public ownership of the means of production, would have been impossible. So the first step of this transformation of a society is based on political action, even if the original motivation may be an economic one. In the first stage of the social and economic development of the new socialist system, nearly every policy, and economic policy in particular, is subject to a very rigid central control in order to strengthen the political and social regime. In the economic sphere, the logical consequence is the introduction of overall planning together with the creation of new centralized institutions, which supervise and intervene in almost the whole economic activity of the country. Those new institutions, mainly the Planning Office or Commission, have as their main task the elaboration down to the smallest detail of targets for every economic unit – in industrial and agricultural production, internal and foreign trade, transport, education, health, etc. This is how the strict and rigid centralized planning of the national economy originated. One has further to take into account that those planning and management methods originate at a time when socialist production relations are still inadequately developed and the level of productive forces relatively low. They are the inevitable corollary of a situation when raw materials are in short supply and mostly have to be distributed among the key enterprises by administrative methods, and when the average level of managerial training and experience still leaves much to be desired. To a greater or lesser extent, this was the case in all the European socialist countries.

Thus nearly all questions of production and capital construction have been decided at the centre. The planning bodies often relieved production executives of the need to decide even minor questions, forgetting their intermediary role and losing sight of the big problems involved in working out optimal plans.

Centralization helped to accelerate the social and structural reconstruction of the economy and to ensure progress along socialist lines at a time when the class composition of the managerial personnel was undergoing a radical change, and it facilitated rapid economic equalization between various regions of the countries concerned. In introducing strict centralized planning and management, there is however always the danger that such a system will become overwhelmingly bureaucratic, functioning in consequence in an administrative rather than an economic way.

Rigid centralized planning, which does not necessarily mean bureaucratic and administrative planning, seems necessary in the period of transition from capitalism to socialism, even in the first stage of the development of a socialist economy. Without centralized planning, even a restructuralization of the economy, in particular the building up of an industry producing the means of production, seems impossible. In this period, the autonomy of production units must be necessarily very limited.

Under the old form of planning and management, investments financed by the socialist state (which centralized the depreciation funds and savings of enterprises) went into expanding production facilities, i.e. building new factories and producing and installing additional machines. The logical consequence was that resources were becoming scarcer and scarcer for the renewal and the modernization of *existing* plants and installations, and the whole infra-structure. The new fixed assets, however, did not compensate for the diminishing returns caused by obsolescence in the old plants. As a result investments, despite their steady growth, proved less and less effective. The result in almost all socialist countries was a certain disproportion between the rate of growth of national income and increments in the volume of fixed assets. This disproportion was extreme in Czechoslovakia.

A further problem was labour. For a time it was possible to maintain the rate of growth of labour by drawing on available labour power among housewives and enlisting in the industrial labour force people formerly employed in agriculture and other branches, unfortunately mostly taken from service industries. But when these auxiliary sources were exhausted, it became more imperative than ever to place the emphasis on higher productivity.

Another problem has been the unfavourable trend in the production structure, both the 'macro-structure' – the proportions between branches of industry – and the 'micro-structure' – the relation between the output of various items within each branch.[1]

There has been also some discrepancy between the interests of the society and those of the various economic units; this is a consequence of rigid administrative planning and management methods. For example, the interests of society demanded that the plan of each enterprise should be optimal, while the interests of the managerial and executive personnel at the point of production prompted them to keep their production programmes down so as to ensure bonuses for overfulfilment. These tendencies resulted from the whole conception of a planning system based primarily on quantitative indexes. One of the most important shortcomings from the theoretical point of view was the ideological argument, laid down by the late Joseph Stalin, that the law of value is a survival of capitalism and hence essentially alien to socialism.

For all those main reasons, the economies of almost all socialist countries developed in a way which could be called extensive rather than intensive. The existing system of rigid administrative planning and management was unable to overcome the contradiction between trends in production and in consumption, and it was at the same time deepening the discrepancies between the structure of production and the structure of demand. The one-sided drive for more output, for quantitative targets, is inevitably accompanied by a lack of incentive for technical and technological advance.

As technical and technological advance is the 'alpha and omega' of every modern society, and as socialist countries are not living in a vacuum, but are an integrated part of the world economy, it was no longer possible to stand by without searching for new methods and measures to

[1] See O. Sik, *Economic Planning and Management in Czechoslovakia*, Prague 1966, p. 6.

overcome the disequilibrium in the national economy. The present system leaves no room for the introduction of modern and efficient techniques, or innovations. So we have to understand the changes in planning and management in the sixties in almost all European socialist countries as an expression of the need to prevent further disequilibrium in their economies, and also as the result of the technological evolution which has been taking place in the most advanced industrialized countries.

Both economic research and practical experience under the actual economic and social conditions in the majority of European socialist countries show that the best mechanism for the further development of the national economy is the interdependence of socialist planning and the socialist market. Let me explain what should be understood by a 'socialist market'. In the first place, one has to bear in mind the basic fact that the socialist system reached already in its first stage a broad socialisation of production relations, which was further extended until the whole economy was and is characterized by social relations of production. Having reached this relatively high stage of socialisation, the level of the productive *forces* was not able – precisely as one of the main results of strict administrative planning and management – to make enough progress for this socialization of the production *relations*.

In the most advanced industrialized Western countries one can see exactly opposite trends. An enormous development of the productive forces, the further growth of which is hampered by the relative backwardness of production relations, is mostly represented by private ownership. Of course, in recent years one cannot overlook the fact that, in the most advanced Western countries, some socialization of the productive relations has taken place. Summarizing, in the European socialist countries a high level of socialization of production relations goes with a relatively lower level of productive forces; in the most advanced Western countries, a high level of productive forces can be found together with a lower level of the organization of production relations. In both systems, the consequent disequilibrium provokes difficulties for further economic and even social development.

To avoid aggravating the disequilibrium, the economies of the socialist countries realized that the socialist market should operate as a very important and efficient corrective to the distortions of the previous years, which had resulted from rigid administrative planning and management.

A socialist economy is generally characterized by the form and the extent of the socialization of its production relations. As agriculture is also covered – socialization in agriculture ranged between 14 and 90 per cent in different countries – the socialist market consists mainly of socialist production, distribution and service units. There is, in principle, no private sector except agriculture in some socialist countries, and naturally the physical consumer of final consumer goods. Those operating on the socialist market are therefore, in principle, all socialist enterprises. Production units can enter in the market either as suppliers or as buyers or in both capacities. The same is true of all kinds of services which, however, tend to be purchasers *vis-à-vis* productive enterprises and suppliers *vis-à-vis* private consumers.

The new planning and management system takes into account the influence of forces on the socialist market, forces which have always existed but have been systematically underestimated and even neglected in the past.

One of the basic aspects of the economic reform now being implemented in some degree in almost all European socialist countries is the combination of centralized leadership and planning with the active role of the market and commodity-money relations. Instead of rigid regulation and control over enterprises, a flexible system of self-regulation is being created, making it possible to gear production programmes to consumer demand and to make the most rational use of resources.

The object of state planning is basically a dual one: ensuring the proper balance in social investment and the optimal use of all production and human resources. Both tasks have aspects in the general economic plane and specifically in production. Many nationwide and inter-branch (and some internal) balances in the various industries can be regulated only on a national scale, in a centralized way. At the same time, priorities bearing, e.g. on the range of consumer goods, the types and sizes of rolled metal, the technical specifications of machines and tools, and other matters of direct interest to the buyer, can be determined by the various branches of industry or even by individual enterprises.

Optimal planning is complicated by the fact that, with the growth and consolidation of the economy, the number of possible variants in both the production and the consumption spheres is multiplying rapidly. Who is to choose the best variant and on what criteria should the choice be based?[1]

It seems essential that a strict demarcation line must be drawn between the functions of central bodies and those of the enterprises.

[1] R. Belousov, *The Plan and the Market in the Socialist Economy*, Prague 1967 p. 103.

Only a central body is able to ensure, through a long-range plan, the relative rates of development and the necessary structural changes in the economy. The long-range plan deals primarily with basic capital investment in conformity with the macro-structural requirements, the main trend of technological progress, the volume and output of the most important items, especially those in short supply, consistency between international division of labour and the national economy (primarily from the standpoint of fulfilling long-term agreements with other socialist countries), the perspectives as regards the structure of the labour force and its skills, and, lastly, the main trends in the distribution of the national income which determines the basic economic proportions.[1]

Concerning the self-regulation of enterprises, the best mechanisms to influence their decision-making are the market, commodity-money relations, organically integrated with cost accounting and material incentives. In this way the interests of the enterprises and those of society should be harmonized by the overall state plan, augmented by a system of 'economic rules' and levers connected with commodity-money relations.

In contrast to the previous period, the state plan can no longer be an administrative, directive one. No longer can obligatory production indicators be established from above by the central body for subordinate managers. Instead, the macro-economic objectives should be achieved by issuing guide-lines providing the lower levels with adequate information. It seems obvious that socially necessary production can be more effectively promoted by cutting down on the number of obligatory targets set from above, and the enterprises should find it in their interest to choose production targets meeting the needs of society and the national economy. Enterprises have to be provided with incentives not only to increase output and raise productivity but also to improve quality. It follows that enterprises, i.e. their directors, should be able to exert direct influence on the construction of the two-year, five-year or long-range plans and forecasts, so that these plans are consistent with their own. They, not the central planning body, have immediate contact with the market.

There always exists the 'voluntarist' view that a state plan can solve all problems without taking account of economic laws. Not everyone takes a sober view of the real possibilities of planning, some believing that it can embrace and directly regulate all economic transactions and all the diverse economic relationships in the country.

[1] O. Sik, *op. cit.*, p. 16.

There are a number of objective reasons why it is not possible – for the time being at least – to foresee in detail the structure of the economy, especially for long periods ahead. For instance, there is no natural growth rate of scientific and technological discoveries, nor is it possible to tell precisely when new types of machines or consumer goods will make their appearance. Hence one must either base plans on existing designs and technology (and this often retards technological progress), or leave these questions open for the time being. Analogous problems arise over prospecting for minerals. A specific difficulty is agriculture, because of its extreme dependence on weather conditions. Finally, there is the difficulty of estimating the income elasticity of demand for consumer goods.

In all these areas more or less accurate prognostications are of course possible, but they are subject to adjustments in the course of the plan's operation. Under those conditions it is precisely the socialist market, the commodity-money relations, which can be effectively used to make state guidance of the economy more flexible, to harmonize production with consumption. Today the mobilization of resources is no longer the main question, but their optimal utilization.

Further, the pace of technological revolution requires that producers adjust their programmes in keeping with it. Here, too, the market comes to the aid of centralized planning. The promotion of trade in the objects and instruments of labour, plus proper price formation and material incentives, provides a powerful stimulus to keeping the production programme in step with the times, while making it possible to supply, without bureaucracy and various administrative measures, the raw materials and equipment needed to turn out new types of machines. Enhancing the role of trade heightens the influence exerted by the consumer on production. So far this is one of the best ways of exercising control over quality and stimulating the output of technologically more advanced goods at lower costs.

A further reason for greater emphasis on the role of commodity-money relations is the need to make production more sensitive to changes in market conditions when supply and demand are in approximate balance. In the past – and even now – when the balance between supply and demand was disrupted, everything on sale was easily sold. More recently, however, owing to the relatively higher average individual income, demand is concentrated on products of higher quality and the production is not always able to cover this change in the composition of demand. Mostly this has been – and more or less is so even now – the case in light industry, where stocks of many items showed excessive growth. In heavy industry, where technical supplies and materials are provided through centralized channels, this phenomenon made itself felt indirectly, primarily in the slower launching of new products and insufficiently rapid improvement of quality. This is one of the reasons why even technical supplies and materials should be incorporated in the commodity-money relations, not only consumer goods.

In order to understand the essence of the socialist market it is necessary to remember that, as an important complement to the plan, market regulation of production is effected under the overall control of the state. The plan and the market are inter-connected and mutually conditioned economic categories. The dependence of the market on the plan is obvious, but at the same time a plan which does not take cognisance of the market is a bad one.

As has been already mentioned, an important question is the balance between supply and demand. In practice this means that the total volume of commodities offered should be sold and that the consumer should be able to buy everything he needs. In other words the proceeds from sales should correspond to the value actually created and realized, while relative prices should correspond to the socially necessary expenses of production. In the framework of the new planning and management, prices are supposed to acquire an additional function. They should help to channel production along lines which are valuable for the whole of society. Fixing of prices should be flexible in accordance with offer and demand. The wider the range of output in a given socialist economy, the more flexible prices will be, and the more inappropriate for them to be fixed by one central body. From this point of view, the method of price formation differs in various socialist countries. In Czechoslovakia for instance the new system of management provides three categories of prices: fixed prices, limited prices and free prices.

'Fixed prices' will be set by the central planning body for the most important items – the principal raw materials, fuel, electric power, major types of machinery and industrial equipment, staple foods and manufactured consumer goods. For goods in the 'limited price' category, the central body will set the maximum and minimum limits within which the supplying plant fixes the sale price, by mutual agreement with buyers. The third group takes in articles of minor importance from the standpoint of economic progress and standard of living; here the prices are to be set by agreement between the supplying plant and purchasing enterprises, or determined by supply and demand.

There are of course also other measures within the combined system of plan and market, to achieve a balance between supply and demand. For instance, by increasing prices. But such a measure could be considered as only an auxiliary one; if productivity of labour is not increasing fundamentally, then a general increase of prices will have no effect on the further development of the economy, indeed the contrary.

It is obvious that the combined system of plan and market involves, because enterprises are entrusted with more liberty of action, an important decentralization and democratization of the national economy. Economics, however, is not a discipline isolated from other social activities. If people are expected to make economic decisions in a more or less independent way, this will necessarily change their behaviour, and the change cannot and will not be limited to economics only. These democratic trends must necessarily penetrate to the whole political and social life of the society, of course as a specifically socialist democracy.

In summarizing, one could consider the recent economic reforms in almost all European socialist countries as the result of a certain disequilibrium of the economy and the evident need for the introduction of new technological processes – they are measures based primarily on economic considerations but needing realization by political decision.

In connection with the economic reforms in the socialist countries, consisting in a sort of synthesis between plan and market, a new question arises. This combination of plan and market seems to be a definitive solution – in as far as in our world anything is definitive! Is the market, especially in a highly developed economy – socialist or capitalist – supplanting planning, or is the plan suppressing the market, or are they both complementing each other?

Speaking very generally, we are witnessing in both systems – capitalist and socialist – very strong tendencies leading to a vertical integration in both industry and agriculture. A vertical integration or co-operation consists in principle in uniting several production units dealing with the same product at various stages of the production process into one unit. This unit comprises then all the stages of production, beginning for example, with the extractive industry and finishing with the distribution of the final product. J. K. Galbraith said in another connection that in a modern industrial society every enterprise is obliged to plan: 'from the time and capital that must be committed, the inflexibility to this commitment, the needs of large organization and the problems of market performance under conditions of advanced technology, comes the necessity of planning'.[1] He continues: '... the firm must take every feasible step to see that what it decides to produce is wanted by the consumer at a remunerative price. . . . And it must see that the labour, materials and equipment that it needs will be available at a cost consistent with the price it will receive. It must exercise control over what is sold. It must exercise control over what is supplied. It must replace the market with planning.'[2] Mr Galbraith expresses the opinion that high technology and heavy capital use cannot be subordinate to market oscillations,[3] so that in his opinion planning must replace the market. He adds that 'in the Soviet type economies the control of prices is a function of the state. . . . Large-scale industrialism requires, in both cases (Western and socialist) that the market and consumer sovereignty be extensively superseded'.[4]

It is a matter of fact that planning is today common in the Western economies also. There is in general, however, a difference between planning in socialist and capitalist economies. For the former is characteristically macro-economic planning, for the latter the basis of planning is micro-economic. So, in other words, in the socialist economy the state is planning, in the capitalist economy it is the private owner, the production unit, the enterprise, the monopoly as a whole, even if there are a number of cases where state plans are in operation and implemented. Higher technology leads to further specialization in both systems, to higher efficiency. Higher technology demands planning, and very often long-range planning. Almost all modern forms of productive technology need important investments, beginning with research and design, and the construction of the plant, up to the production process and distribution.

In the most advanced Western industrialized countries – the United States, the EEC members, United Kingdom and Japan – big firms are indeed not only planning the production programmes, but also, by detailed investigations of the market, they try to influence the latter with the aim of regulating supply and demand. The more the big corporations or monopolies in capitalist countries concentrate in their own hands (through vertical and horizontal integration) the economy of a country, and particularly if they influence (by international economic integration) production and marketing in various countries, the more they will be able to elaborate plans of production and consumption, even for several units. If we add to this observation, the fact that

---

[1] J. K. Galbraith, *The New Industrial State*, London 1967, p. 16.
[2] *Ibid.*, pp. 23, 24.   [3] *Ibid.*, p. 319.   [4] *Ibid.*, pp. 389, 390.

in the most industrialized Western countries the leading corporations and monopolies are deeply involved in national and international politics in the framework of the activities of the governments, then it seems that Mr Galbraith's assumption that the market will be suppressed by the planning of the monopolies cannot be excluded for the longer-term future, provided that technological progress will not be limited to some sectors of the economy only.

Does it not seem in the light of the above observation anachronistic that the socialist countries are introducing just now, as a fundamentally new approach, the combination between plan and market? I believe this is not so at all, mainly because the previous administrative and directive method of planning and management must become much more flexible. The change to flexibility in planning cannot be achieved by administrative decisions but must be regulated by economic factors, by commodity-money relations, by the market. Further, the function of planning in socialist countries differs from that in capitalist countries as has been shown already. In socialist countries the setting up of a national economic plan of development is at the same time a political act influencing the whole society, in every social aspect. That is why the greater economic independence of enterprises and the development of commodity-money relations in no way imply passive submission to the requirements of the market. Even if, due to technological progress, the organization of production and consumption should follow the same lines as seems to be the case in the most advanced capitalist countries, e.g. by vertical and horizontal integration, whatever this organization will be, these integrated enterprises will always be socialist enterprises, guided by an overall national plan.

It may be that, in the future, if the intensification of socialist production relations will go further and socialist countries will be able to create a society of abundance, improvement of scientific aspects of planning, including the mechanization and automation of the processing of information and computer operations, will gradually lead to an effective and flexible system of regulating the production process without the agency of the market. Economic information will flow through special communication channels from consumers and producers to centres forming an integrated directing body. Here the information will be processed by electronic machines to produce an economico-mathematical model showing the entire economy and its future prospects, as well as a general picture of the reciprocal links basic to optimal ratios of social production and consumption. In this way production will be effectively regulated, while leaving a certain freedom for amalgamations and enterprises to display initiative and, consequently, to regulate their own performance, not under the impact of the market, but on the basis of the impulses generated by development.[1]

The transition to a system of this type is dependent on such objective factors as the maturity of society and the level of productive forces. Whether and when human society, and in particular society in socialist states, will reach this stage of development will become clear in time. We are not so far from this stage now. While no better mechanism is created, commodity-money relations, the market, combined with central planning, can be effectively used to harmonize production with consumption.

[1] R. Belousov, *op. cit.*, p. 107.

Discussion of Professor Arnost Tauber's Paper

Opening the discussion Mr Lipton said that Professor Tauber's paper reflected the 'convergence thesis', that there is increasing similarity between economic organizations in the capitalist and socialist countries. The question was whether this convergence had any lessons for the less developed countries; and specifically, to what extent price policy has a role in less developed countries which are committed in various degrees to central planning. Mr Lipton then summarized the main arguments for and against the use of price policy as opposed to physical controls.

On the positive side, there is known to be price-responsiveness in the less developed economies. Earlier arguments that peasants will not respond to prices were mistaken and one of the main objections to price policy has been shown to be illusory. It is suggested that having shown that the necessary conditions for price policy exist it should be used.

Second, systems of direct control are open to misuse – particularly through corruption (which is a consequence of poverty). Direct controls are also misused under 'pseudo-planning' where 'plans' are essentially intended as ideological protection for rich ruling groups. Whatever the weaknesses and biases of the price system they are likely to have less harmful consequences than the abuse of direct control.

Third, planned development puts heavy pressure on the civil servants, who are expected to give up their function as guardians of the *status quo* and implement complex and radical changes. Price policies make fewer demands upon them than administrative controls.

There are, however, some arguments against a rapid switch to exclusive reliance on price policy by less developed countries. The communist model might be as misleading here as in its earlier use, to concentrate on physical planning and lop-sided heavy-industrialization. COMECON countries like Czechoslovakia had been forced to meet their problem, of excess supply of some goods and deficient supply of others, by a lunge towards pricing. This was because the usual alternative – to export their surplus goods and buy their deficient goods – was not open to them to any great extent; partly because of legally binding COMECON arrangements, partly because such extra exports as were possible – to the USSR – involved production lines and processes implying severe technological backwardness. These special circumstances did not exist in less developed countries, and the arguments for advising them to correct supply-demand imbalances by international trade, and not by domestic pricing, should be considered.

Mr Lipton felt that there were contradictions between the two versions of price policy discussed in Professor Tauber's paper and used in practice in Czechoslovakia. Professor Tauber described the Czechoslovak system as having free prices for certain goods and fixed prices for others. Mr Lipton suggested that there were inconsistencies in this policy, that one might have a price policy or one might use the price mechanism, but that it was very difficult to do both things at the same time, particularly where there is a high degree of substitution between the goods in question, and between the factors used in their production. For example, rising prices for items in the 'free price mechanism' sector could bid up the values of competitive items (or items using similar factors) in the 'fixed price policy' sector, and distort incentives to both buyers and sellers.

Secondly, the basic question in price policy, i.e. in fixing prices, is to work out what prices one wants. This may be a particularly difficult exercise where there is a lack of statistical information and a lack of people who can interpret it.

Thirdly, in most less developed countries, there is an inherent tendency for priorities to be biased towards the requirements of the urban communities. This is partly a political matter, but it also results from the relative strength of public ownership in the urban industrial sector which makes planning easier there, and also results in a tendency to plan for the urban sector. Price policies have to be measured against other policies in terms of their relative effectiveness in correcting these biases. Mr Lipton noted that price policy has been used against the rural sector in order to ensure cheap food supply; in heavy protection for industry alone; in pricing farm inputs like fertilizers; and in selectively giving cheap credit to bigger farmers who supply food to the towns.

In the further discussion, other arguments were put against relying on price policies in development planning. It was argued that the role of price policies is to separate the function of price in influencing demand from its function in influencing supply; but, practically speaking, whilst prices may be useful in influencing demand, it was doubtful whether they were an effective way of influencing supply. As far as price policy works it influences relative prices. If, on the other hand, price increases become cumulative, the overall effects will simply be inflationary. Here rationing may be preferable even though it also has some inflationary effects. Again, there was some doubt about the efficacy of large short-term adjustments in price in influencing supply in desired ways. Temporary shortages might be better met by choosing some medium price between the long- and short-term prices.

In addition, it was pointed out that price policy means that the market has to be 'run'. Running the market, however, makes heavy demands for information and for experience and both these are lacking in the normal case. There are major problems of distinguishing temporary from permanent price changes, and irreversible from reversible changes. In addition, price policy means that planners have to work with uncertainties which are not present if direct controls are used.

It was also agreed that there were some specific problems about using price policy in less developed countries. For example, the developmental problems in Latin America were very different from those in Eastern Europe and may not be accessible to the same kinds of policy. The Latin American economies are characterized by slow accumulation of capital, unequal income distribution, severe structural imbalances and foreign dependence. The solution to many of these problems involve serious questions of resource allocation, but whether price policies could affect the desired solutions was questionable.

Finally, it was suggested that there were some distinctive characteristics of less developed economies which suggest a modification of the arguments in favour of price policies. In particular the inevitable openness of the less developed economies (their comparative advantage lies in importing machinery), the low investment ratios and the tendency to labour surplus were mentioned. In this context it is useful to distinguish between factor price policies and commodity price policies; the former might be a more useful weapon. The problem is to set prices for labour, capital and foreign exchange which reflect relative availabilities – and not so much to set commodity prices *per se*.

In the discussion on the applicability of Eastern European planning experience to the less developed countries, it was argued that there were dangers in attempting piecemeal applications of the Soviet model. In order to have an effective planning mechanism one must pay the price, which might be quite high. The conditions which would have to be met to apply Soviet-type planning were enumerated. First, there must be conscious political willingness and administrative capability to plan. These conditions would be met under the form of political organization called the dictatorship of the proletariat. Second, there must be a high degree of public control. Third, there had to be a nation-wide administrative machinery; and finally, there must be a comprehensive medium- and long-term perspective. Planning means optimization and if there are no optimizing procedures there is no real planning.

Finally, there were comments and questions on the development of planning in Eastern Europe. Some points additional to Professor Tauber's analysis were made. In particular the 'over-determined' character of most centralized plans was described. There were examples in Eastern Europe where gross output targets measured in currency units did not correspond to the fixed price values of the physical output targets. In addition, there were problems where raw materials were scarce and accordingly might be rationed on an average basis within sectors. In these circumstances enterprises which did not actually need the materials in question would often hold stocks 'just in case'. Centralized planning was bureaucratic as well as centralized and had been demoralizing to factory managers.

The question was also raised whether the use of material incentives would not undermine the social relations which had been established.

Chapter Seven

PLANNING IN YUGOSLAVIA

Professor Branko Horvat

I. Introduction

As an independent national state Yugoslavia was created only half a century ago, in 1918. The first five decades have been rather turbulent, as one would expect for a Balkan country. Modern writers on comparative economic systems distinguish three different socio-economic systems coexisting today: capitalist, centrally planned and associationist (market socialist, labour managed, self-governing).[1] The last mentioned represents a class with a single member: Yugoslavia. For better or worse the present generation of this country – economists included – has had a unique opportunity to try out all three economic systems mentioned and also all imaginable political systems. This may help to explain a lot of what is now happening in the country.

This same generation has also lived through three different stages of economic development: pre-industrial, developing and the now beginning industrialized stage. Pre-war Yugoslavia was a poor agricultural country with peasants representing almost 80 per cent of the population, and with almost one half of the population illiterate. The rate of growth was low, 3·1 per cent per annum for the period 1920-39; social product *per capita* grew at an average rate of 1·7 per cent.[2] Today the Yugoslav economy produces on *per capita* basis almost as much as the French economy in 1938,[3] peasants represent less than one half of the

[1] Cf. G. Grossman, *Economic Systems*, New York, 1967.

[2] I. Vinski, 'Nacionalni dohodak i fiksni fondovi na podrucju Jugoslavije 1909-1959', *Ekonomski pregled*, 11-12, 1959, p. 837.

[3] If French figures are reduced by factor 2·11 to account for the difference in population size, the following comparison may serve as an illustration

	France (adjusted) 1938	Yugoslavia 1965
Electric power generation, billions of KWh	9·9	15·5
Steel, millions of tons	3·0	1·8
Cement, millions of tons	2·0	4·0
Grain, millions of tons	8·4	10·6

(*UN Statistical Yearbook*, 1951, *SGJ*-1966)

population and social product expands at a rate of 7·7 per cent *per capita* annually.

The Yugoslav institutional model

It may be helpful to describe briefly the institutional structure of the Yugoslav economy as it has evolved until now. The last phrase is not

Figure 1. Institutional Model of the Jugoslav Economic System

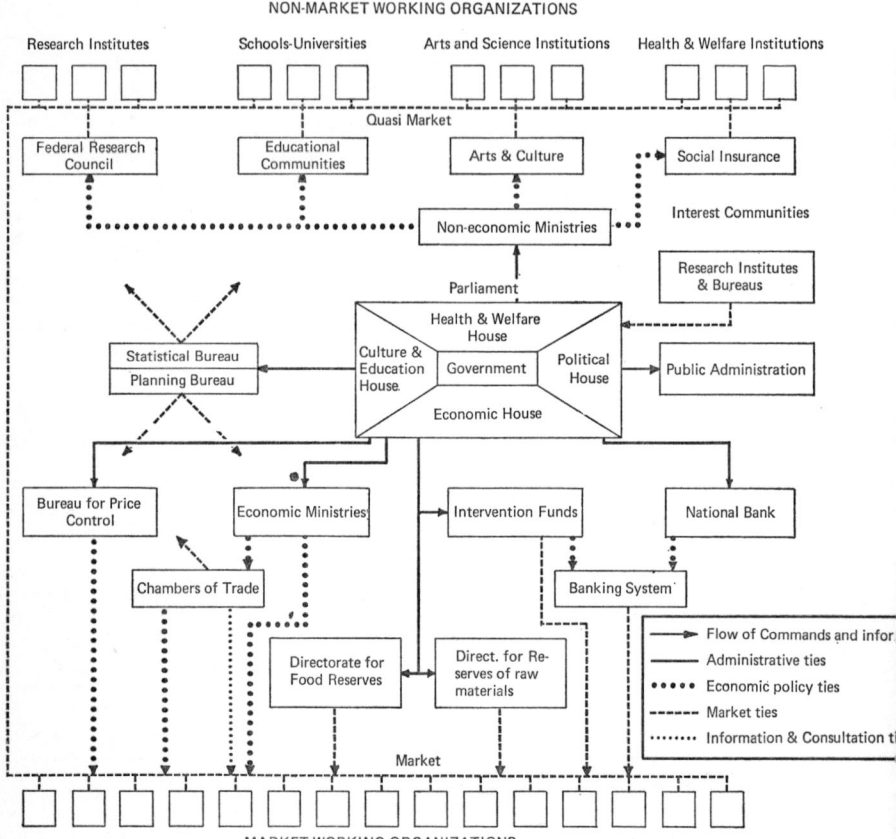

accidental: the system is still in flux and each year brings new changes. A somewhat simplified picture of the Yugoslav institutional model is given in Figure 1. The names of certain institutions may sound awkward in English translation, since interlingual untranslatability is frequent with highly specific socio-economic development.

The Yugoslav economic system consists of autonomous, self-governing, working organizations[1] and individual producers in market and non-market sectors and of government machinery. The task of the latter is to use *non-administrative* means in co-ordinating the activities of market and non-market agents and to organize public administration in certain fields of common interest (judiciary, defence, foreign affairs, etc.).

The functioning of this economic system is based on the assumptions that self-governing collectives are materially interested in maximizing their incomes and that the Government and the Parliament are able to create an economic environment in which autonomous decision makers behave in accordance with general social interests. Both assumptions seem to have been proved by modern theory of economic policy and by experience in decentralized market economy. Between the 'Center' (Parliament) and the 'Periphery' (working organizations) four types of gravitational forces are active, keeping the system in equilibrium and the economic agents on the predictive trajectories of social interest. These forces are information – consultation ties, market ties, economic policy ties (instruments of economic policy and legislature) and administrative ties. The last mentioned are exceptional as far as economic agents are concerned and apply to various organs of the Center such as ministries, National Bank, certain bureaux and the like.

There is also a fifth type of tie – political ties – which closes the whole structure connecting the working organizations with the Parliament and with flows of commands (arrows) oriented from Periphery towards Center. In order to keep this paper short, I shall not analyse these ties (this is why they are left out of Figure 1). It is, however, important to realize that the Parliament is organized in a rather unorthodox fashion. Apart from the traditional Political House, whose members are more or less professional politicians, elected by all citizens, there are three additional houses, dealing with three different social-economic groups of problems (economic, health and welfare, education and culture). The members of these three 'Houses of Working Organizations' are not professionals, they keep their usual jobs and are elected by 'producers' in these three specific fields. It may be of some interest to note that the Yugoslav Parliamentary system resembles – at that time

[1] 'Working organization' is a constitutional term meant to underline a fundamental equality in rights and status of every group of citizens organized with an intention to earn their living regardless of the activity they perform. An enterprise, a theatre and a government office – all of them are working organizations.

considered Utopian – the ideas of the late G. D. H. Cole and his Guild
Socialists.[1]

Let us now have a look at the market half of our economic cosmos.
The activities of enterprises and individual producers[2] are co-ordinated
by the market in the first place. The market is, however, a very rough
and unreliable mechanism requiring constant adjustments. These adjustments are achieved through general regulative measures and instruments of economic policy of the Government. The financial flows, intended to achieve desirable allocation of resources, are regulated by the
National Bank within the framework of the Social Plan. There are two
additional types of specific financial interventions: in the field of foreign
trade (credits and exchange insurance) and investment (ensuring proper
structure and regional allocation of capital formation). These three purposes are served by three federal funds: for export credits, for under-
developed regions and for investment.

Market equilibrium is being worked upon by three institutions. Two
of them – directorates for food and for industrial products reserves –
intervene whenever supply and demand do not match. The former
directorate also administers agricultural support prices. The third institution – the Price Control Bureau – is now a somewhat alien element to
the system. I expect that in the near future this governmental bureau
will evolve into a Price and Wage Arbitrage, an institution in which all
relevant interests are represented and all decisions made jointly. At the
moment more than 40 per cent of industrial prices are controlled.

Statistical and Planning Bureaux have only informative-consultative
functions in this system.

A rather peculiar arrangement of the Yugoslav system is to be found
in what I call a *quasi market*. The activities of schools, hospitals,
museums, and other non-market working organizations cannot be co-
ordinated by the market directly as is done in the case of enterprises.
In a socialist society sick persons should be healed, talented youths
educated, regardless of whether and how much they can afford to pay.
On the other hand, the traditional budget financing of non-market
activities has led to bureaucratic practices incompatible with a self-

---

[1] Cf. for instance G. D. H. Cole, *Guild Socialism Re-stated*, London 1920.
[2] It is of some importance to realize that individual producers (the so-called
private sector) do not represent an alien element in the Yugoslav system as they
do in a centrally planned economy. In connection with this one should also
realize that the dichotomy 'state-private' is not related to the dichotomy
'socialist-capitalist'. For an extensive discussion see B. Horvat, *An Essay on
Yugoslav Society*, I.A.S.P., New York 1969.

government system. The solution of this dilemma was sought in an interpolation of a special self-government mechanism between the government and the non-market working organizations. This mechanism is called interest communities. The communities obtain their financial resources on the basis of parliamentary decisions and then buy services of non-market producers on behalf of the society. The non-market producers compete for available resources by offering their services on differential conditions. In this way there emerges a special type of market – a quasi market – which makes it possible for the relations between the non-market sector and the society to be economically conditioned, for the collectives in the non-market sector to preserve their self-government, autonomy, and at the same time for relations within the fields of education, culture and social welfare to be based on the principle of 'distribution according to needs', which is one of the preconditions of a socialist society. It is clear that the enterprises can also intervene in the non-market sector – either by buying services directly or by creating special foundations – and that is why in Figure 1 market and non-market sectors are also directly connected by market ties.

Apart from economic relations between federal bodies and economic agents there are relations between federal and state and local authorities, between the latter two and the working organizations and among all of them. I must, however, skip the description of all these relations, although they are extremely important for the functioning of the system as a whole.

II. Construction of a Plan

Political interest in planning

It is rather axiomatic that a socialist economy is to be planned. Therefore, it is rather obvious that planning involves political interests. The actual planning practices in Yugoslavia have passed through three different stages.

Before the war there was no planning – a situation not uncommon for the rest of the world. Immediately after the revolution, 1945-47, the country adopted the only then available planning model, the Soviet model of a command economy with central planning. The Soviet practices were followed very closely. Since they are by now well known, I need not dwell upon them. The results were not overly encouraging. The output and employment did rise considerably, but productivity increase was modest, and technological progress was even negative as measured by standard methods.[1] Excessive and wrongly structured investment produced negative marginal efficiency of investment. As a consequence consumption was unnecessarily low. The attempts at collectivization kept agriculture stagnant. But most important were the evidently negative political consequences of complete bureaucratization of the economy. These developments were clearly not in line with the ideals of the Revolution and the command economy had to be transformed into something more desirable.

In 1950 workers' councils were introduced. A year later a decentralization process began. The market was gaining in importance. In 1952 administrative planning began to be gradually replaced by what was called 'planning of global proportions'. By 1960 the planning practices were very similar to French indicative planning.

After 1960 a search for new and more adequate methods for organizing the self-governing economy began. In 1961 a reform was undertaken, but failed. In 1963 the new Constitution – containing important innovations like the concept of the working organization – was passed in Parliament. Two years later a new and more radical reform was attempted. The reform did not prove successful economically, but it triggered a process of extremely important political and social changes. Three D's – Decentralization, Democratization and De-étatization – became part and parcel of the establishment. A search for economic framework, appropriate for the suddenly enormously increased complexity of the society, is still going on. And the period 1960-69 may be adequately described as a period of crisis in planning.

The size and place of planning offices

In 1960 the Federal Planning Bureau had a staff of about 160, somewhat more than one half of whom were professionals, mostly engineers. Each of the six states and two autonomous provinces had its own planning bureau. The same applies to cities and other administrative units. Planning bureaux are professional consulting institutions to their respective authorities and have no administrative powers. As a consequence, no hierarchy exists; there are no lines of subordination in planning. From time to time representatives from the state bureaux meet with their colleagues in the federal bureau in order to keep track of and coordinate the work they do; similar meetings are repeated on lower levels. The decisions of these meetings are not binding unless unanimous. And

[1] B. Horvat, 'Technological Progress in Yugoslavia', *Economic Analysis*, Issue No. 1-2, 1969.

even then it is not quite clear what would be the consequences of failure to comply. Differences of opinion are settled on political levels among respective governments.

The Federal Planning Bureau – and similarly the state bureaux used to have three different divisions: for sectoral projections, for co-ordinative planning and for administrative services. The first division had the following departments: manufacturing and mining; agriculture and fishing; forestry, building and construction; transportation and communications; trade and catering. Co-ordinative planning was concerned with personal and government consumption and living standards, manpower projections, investment, foreign trade, regional development and overall co-ordination; the last activity was located in the National Income Department. This scheme, which existed for about a decade – an unusually long period in the Yugoslav environment – was later extended to include problems of prices and financial flows. However, the work in these two fields has never been developed in a satisfactory way. The Bureau remained primarily an institution of physical planning, evidently still bearing the imprints of the times when it was born. As such it does not fit too well into a developed market economy.

One of the consequences of the decentralization drive intensified by the new Constitution in 1963 was a fair representation of the states in government bodies, including the Federal Planning Bureau. Since there are six states, the Bureau got six directors. To provide work for the new directors, the Bureau was broken into six groups. Since this organization did not prove particularly efficient – as one might have expected on *a priori* grounds – I shall not bother to describe it in detail. Besides, steps have already been taken to reorganize the Bureau in a more efficient way.

Projection framework

The Federal Planning Bureau experimented with two methods of drawing up plans: the sector aggregation method and the breaking down of global targets. As far as the first method is concerned, it turned out that whenever the departments of the Bureau were asked to produce independently their sectoral projections, the sum total of sectoral output proved to be considerably lower and the sum total of sectoral investment necessary to sustain this output considerably higher than the realistic global projections. On the basis of this experience the second method came to be used as a rule.

The construction of a plan begins by applying a simple econometric model[1] in the following way. On the basis of informed judgement and auxiliary projections an interval is estimated within which the possible future global rate of growth is likely to take place. From the global rate of growth by means of regression analysis one derives sectoral rates of growth. The sectors correspond to sector projecting departments (manufacturing and mining; agriculture and fishing; forestry; transport and communications; trade and catering; small industry). Next, one derives the output of non-market sectors. And finally the sectoral and aggregate capital formation necessary to sustain the expected output. The capital formation determines, of course, the output of building and construction trades.

The preliminary target plan is constructed in the National Income Department and handed over to other departments for elaboration. It thus serves as an efficient co-ordination device. The further work on plan construction is a process that does not lend itself to precise description or rigorous phasing. What is involved is a mixture of intuition, experience, rules of thumb, various techniques (rarely sophisticated) known to individual planners and an endless series of consultations. Trade unions, chambers of trade, business associations, big enterprises, central and investment banks, ministries and other governmental organs, state planning bureaux, even research workers are consulted at one stage or another. Political bodies (Government, Central Committee, Parliamentary Committees) intervene more than once, examining the preliminary drafts of the plan. When the final draft is adjusted to accommodate all important interests, it is voted in the Parliament.

The adjustment just mentioned is a curious process. During this process the plan gradually loses its concrete details and shrinks to some sort of declaration. As a consequence, in the last couple of years annual plans have been replaced by parliamentary resolutions.

The role accorded to the private sector

Since there is no state sector in Yugoslav economy, there cannot be a private sector either. There is just one, self-government, sector. There is, however, another important economic distinction, namely the distinction between a family enterprise and the rest. The family enterprise may employ up to five workers that are not family members, but the vast majority of individual producers do not use this opportunity up to the limit or at all.

[1] Cf. B. Horvat, 'A Restatement of a Simple Planning Model with some Examples from Yugoslav Economy', *Sankhya*, Series B, Vol. 23, 1960, 29-48.

The family enterprise is dominant in agriculture and in artisan services, but it is found in other sectors as well. In agriculture about 86 per cent of land and 96 per cent of labour force (but only 72 per cent of output) belongs to family enterprises. The shares of family enterprises (of individual producers in the Yugoslav jargon) in the social product of their respective sectors in 1967 were as follows:

Table One

The Share of Family Enterprise in Social Product of Respective Sectors (in %)

	1952	1966
Agriculture	90	71
Construction	7	20
Transport	—	4
Trade and Catering	—	2
Arts and Crafts	61	37
Market Sector Total	29	29

Sources: *Jugoslavial* 1945-1964, p. 80; *SGJ*-1968, p. 110.

Since small scale operations are characteristic for artisan services, the family enterprise may be expected to stay in this sector for a long time. However, there is not much to be planned in this sector. In agriculture the number of individual peasants and the acreage of land they hold are gradually but continually shrinking. In marketable quantities of output their share is now only 52 per cent. Individual producers enter into various co-operative arrangements with agricultural enterprises. Thus planning in agriculture gradually becomes similar to planning in other branches of the economy.

III. Implementation of Plans

The state of affairs

As already stated, planning bureaux have no administrative powers and no means of economic policy at their disposal. They are professional, consultative organs of the government(s) whose duty is to produce plans, check their implementation and analyse business trends. I may add that the last two items of the program have not been carried out too efficiently. Yugoslav planning bureaux have become famous for constantly forgetting to undertake a comparative analysis of how the planned targets have been fulfilled.

In the history of plan implementation in Yugoslavia one may distinguish three periods. The first Five-Year Plan, 1947-51, was never really fulfilled. The period 1952-56 was a period of transition from the command to the market economy in which only annual plans were produced. The second Five-Year Plan, 1957-61, was fulfilled in four years. This is the golden period of planning and a period of extremely high rates of growth. Since 1960 economic growth has slowed down and economic instability has increased. The two successive medium term plans have been abandoned and the present Five-Year Plan (1966-70) is not likely to be fulfilled. It is of considerable interest to examine what caused this crisis in planning and I shall try to do that briefly in the next section.

If we take the coefficient of variation of annual rates of growth with respect to planned annual rates of growth (interpreted as an average or expected value) as a measure of deviation from the plan target, we get the following picture:

Table Two

Coefficients of Deviation from Plan Targets

	1957-60	1961-64
National Income	0·57	0·59
Manufacturing	0·17	0·59
Agricultural output	0·76	0·64
Export	0·35	0·29
Import	0·52	0·62

Source: Jugoslovenski institut za ekonomska istrazivanja, *Sumarana analiza privrednih kretanja i prijedlozi za ekonomsku politiku*, Beograde, 1968, p. 17.

The high coefficients of deviation from the plan targets in agriculture are explained by the unpredictability of the weather conditions and the dependence of the peasant agriculture on weather conditions. Since agriculture is gradually losing its peasant characteristics, the coefficient of deviations is improving. The enormous increase of unpredictability of manufacturing in the second period is due to increased business fluctuations. The planners have been careful not to formulate numerical targets that would enable their own coefficients of deviation to be measured!

The explanation of the state of affairs

As already mentioned, the post-administrative period can be divided in two distinct sub-periods. There was an acceleration of the rate of growth in the first sub-period and a retardation in the second:

Table Three

Rates of Growth 1952-67

	1952-60	1960-67
Social Product	9·8	6·4
Industrial Output	13·5	8·9
Investment	11·3	1·4
Export	12·1	8·3

Source: *Statistical Yearbooks*

It has also been mentioned that in the second period business instability increased and medium-term plans were not fulfilled. What was the reason?

In the eight-year period 1952-60 the industrial growth of Yugoslavia (13·5 per cent) was third in the world (after Japan with 15·4 per cent and Bulgaria with 14 per cent), agricultural growth was absolutely the highest with 9·33 per cent (matched only by Israel with 9·25 per cent) and so was the expansion of *per capita* social product with 8·8 per cent (followed by Bulgaria with 8·1 per cent and Japan with 7·8 per cent).[1] After 1960 Yugoslav *per capita* growth dropped to fourth place with 7·7 per cent for the period 1952-66 (after Japan with 8·2 per cent, Bulgaria with 8 per cent and Rumania with 7·8 per cent).[1] The lower rates of growth after 1960, as shown in the table above, are almost catastrophic by Yugoslav standards (they generated reforms, unemployment and dissatisfaction), but are still among the highest in the world. This difference in subjective evaluation should be borne in mind in order to understand what is going on.

In just a decade and a half after 1952 agricultural output increased 2·5 times, industrial output close to five times, *per capita* social product almost three times. The whole distance between pre-industrial and industrial society was covered in this short period of time. What it means in terms of more normal developments of some other countries can be seen from Table Four.

Even if all inadequacies of data are taken into consideration, the table seems to suggest the following conclusions. As far as the pioneering countries – Great Britain and the United States – are concerned, the Yugoslav economy is lagging behind by more than a century. This lag is reduced to somewhat more than a generation when the other four European countries are taken as a standard of comparison. Yugoslav economic development itself has been extremely uneven. One world

[1] Z. Popov, 'Osvrt na kretanje privrednog razvoja u svetu sa posebnim prikazom razvoja socijalistickih zemalja', *Economic Analysis*, No. 3-4, 1968, pp. 303-4.

Table Four

Per Capita Income in International Units (IU)

Yugoslavia		France		Belgium		Sweden		Italy		Canada		UK		USA	
Year	IU	Year	IU	Year	IU	Year	IU	Year	IU	Year	IU	Year	IU	Year	IU
1929	95	1820	99	1846	101	1861	96	1902	118	—	—	—	—	—	—
1938	95	—	—	—	—	—	—	—	—	—	—	—	—	—	—
1948	107	—	—	—	—	—	—	—	—	—	—	—	—	—	—
1952	97														
1966	271	1913	266	1895	219	1914	276	1953	265	1870	230	1870	325	1850	362
		1928	406	1913	314	1922	268			1880	256			—	—
		1938	366	1927	262	1928	333			1890	341				

Source: For countries other than Yugoslavia; C. Clark, *The Conditions of Economic Progress*, Macmillan, London 1960. One International Unit represents the purchasing power of one dollar in the USA over the decade 1925-34. The estimates for Yugoslavia are obtained by linking *per capita* incomes of Yugoslavia in 1966 with *per capita* income in France in 1938 by an index prepared in the Institute of Economic Sciences by my colleague S. Stajic.

economic depression, one world war and a period of administrative planning cum collectivization *left per capita output stagnant for almost a quarter of a century*. The initiation of self-government in 1950 liberated latent growth potentials and generated an economic explosion in the next decade and a half. Between 1952 and 1966 the development lag of Yugoslavia was reduced as compared with France from 130 years to 53 years, as compared with Belgium from one century to 40 years, as compared with Sweden from 90 years to 44 years, as compared with Italy from half a century to a decade. In other words, the last 14 years of Yugoslavia lasted in France 80 years, in Belgium 60 years, in Sweden 46 years and in Italy somewhat more than 40 years.

Rapid economic development produced difficulties of adjustment. Almost overnight a peasant economy with illiterate population was transformed into an industrialized modern economy with highly complex social institutions. That was too much of a rush for the state apparatus to cope with. Since the problem was not realized in time, things got out of hand. The pace of economic growth was not the only factor of strain. After all, several other countries grew at comparable rates. But, superimposed on economic development were quite radical political and social changes. Yugoslavia was not only to be economically developed but also socially transformed. As I have already mentioned, in this latter respect it turned out (so far) to be the single member of its class. And pioneering is a very exhausting activity.

The state machinery, the institutions, and the individuals in responsible positions began to lag behind the general pace of economic and social development. Many of the old leaders retired, masses of young people were brought to responsible positions, even to top political positions. Rotation of cadres – another socio-political invention – was put to work quite vigorously. But there was a general lack of social experience to cope with continual eruptions of new problems. Two improvised reforms after 1960 made things only worse. The country found itself in the middle of a very turbulent adjustment process. This is what constitutes the crisis of planning in Yugoslavia.

IV. Conclusion

The orientational outline given to me for this paper required that in conclusion an analysis of the effectiveness of planning be given. But that would be a very unnatural ending for a Yugoslav paper. By national temperament we never look backwards, and that is why our planners never evaluate their plans.

Discussion of Professor Branko Horvat's Paper

Mr Skorov remarked that Yugoslavia deserved, more than any other country, the title of a 'social laboratory': it exhibited 'a unique combination of underdevelopment and socialist orientation, lack of democratic tradition and one of the boldest forms of political democracy, multi-national society and a federal structure of government'. It had searched with great determination to give fresh meaning to the old concept of self-government.

On Professor Horvat's characterization of the Yugoslav economy, Mr Skorov questioned the statement that there was no state sector in the economy. Did not national defence, transport, communications, and the central bank constitute such a sector? The use of the term 'family enterprise' was also dubious. If it was allowed that such enterprise could involve the employment of up to five people on a wage basis, in what sense was it wrong to call it 'private enterprise'? Nevertheless, the dominance of collective co-operative ownership justified the claim of Yugoslavia to have a 'socialist' economy.

But, Mr Skorov continued, it was a very distinct form of socialism, relying on the market mechanism to the extent that the term 'socialist market economy' might be appropriate. He doubted the value of the decentralization which was so marked in the Yugoslav structure, feeling that it was responsible for 'irrational decisions, duplication of effort, and waste of resources'.

A scrutiny of the economy's performance confirmed these doubts. Plan targets had not by any means been fulfilled: for the period 1957-60 the 'coefficients of deviation' ranged from 17 per cent to 64 per cent and they had been as high and higher in the period 1961-64. Unemployment was high – higher than it seemed if allowance was made for the considerable migration to Western Europe. Even so, the growth-rate was higher than the rates of many countries in that area. How far, Mr Skorov asked, should the credit for growth be given to the planners? An immediate problem was that of the responsibilities assumed by planners.

Apart from the vagueness in allocation of responsibility between federal and state planning bureaux, the preference shown for indirect controls made Yugoslav planning seem highly 'indicative', if not actually 'permissive': and in comparison French 'indicative' planning seemed 'frightfully authoritarian and "directive"'.

Further, the abandonment of a sectoral aggregative method and the relegation of the Federal Planning Bureau made one doubt whether Yugoslav planning was not, in engineering language, at the design stage rather than engaged in construction. As the preliminary decision about where to build had not been taken, there was no need yet for elaborate technical structures. Yet the lack of machinery for evaluation was disturbing. But, Mr Skorov concluded, those weaknesses should not conceal the enormous achievements of Yugoslavia, which in fifteen years had transformed itself from a poor agrarian society to an early industrial one. The real question remained how much of the credit for this change should be bestowed on the planners, and how much on the revolutionary forces of socialism.

Interesting semantic points arose in the ensuing discussion. One speaker asked rather trenchantly whether socialism as described was not simply capitalism without owners. Another wondered if the so-called 'market' indicated in Professor Horvat's paper really operated in the normally understood sense. A third thought that the atrophying of the Federal Planning Bureau might be abundantly justified by the fact that *everybody* had become planners.

Winding up the discussion, Professor Horvat said that in reality there was only one type of ownership in Yugoslavia, social ownership, because whatever the *size* of the unit, the unit controlled its own business. Units like the army did not count as a public sector because they were extra-economic. But they were still subject to the ethos of self-government.

Chapter Eight

PLANNING IN THE UK

ROGER OPIE

PANACEA; music-hall joke; political anathema. The sequence of attitudes took less than a decade from the end of the Second World War.
The sequence seems likely to repeat itself from 1964 onwards in about
the same length of time.

I deal with this topic under three headings. One, origins; by which
I mean both historical and intellectual. Two, experience of both planning and of non-planning. And three, machinery, which means the
invention of new machinery and the adaptation of old machinery, to
meet both old and new tasks.

Historical and intellectual factors combined in 1961-62 to produce
the foundations of the present planning machinery. This was the first
time in peacetime, a watershed of post-war economic management.

Historically, the idea of economic planning as a type of economic
management derives from the Soviet Union. With highly ideological
overtones, the discussion of planning was naturally political and
emotional rather than technical. The discussions of the thirties were
still at the level of whether a planned socialist system could possibly
be rational. Could prices mean anything without private ownership?

Planning is now ideologically attached to growth. First attempts at
planning by directive were wartime controls. The purpose was a simple
one: to mobilize resources at a time of great shortages for one single
goal irrespective of the consequences in peace. This meant a double shift
of resources, first into the war effort, and then at the end of the war into
exports and investment.

The second planning exercise was planning for balance of payments
equilibrium under the Marshall Plan with a four-year recovery programme for the years 1948-52. Then followed a political and ideological
swing. After wartime and post-war experience came a rediscovery of
the virtues and strengths of the market mechanism, the 'natural order'.
This was especially true in government circles of the day, in both the
new government and the civil service. Planning was at this stage good
for a music-hall joke.

By the end of the 1950s, in a mood of deep disappointment, three factors led to a flirtation with planning. Thus we have a paradox: the government which led the country away from planning at the beginning of the fifties led it back to planning at the beginning of the sixties.

The key factors were: (a) disappointment with the UK's growth performance; (b) disappointment with the traditional weapons of policy; and (c) a theory of growth.

At that time, our growth was in fact accelerating but was very inferior to that of other countries. It was discovered that growth after all was not a by-product of success in other fields of economic management. The philosophy of policy in this period was that of 'arm's length government'. If the economy could be stabilized at about 1·8 per cent unemployment (a new definition of full employment) then stable prices and a stable balance of payments and rapid growth would all follow from this. But instability continued, and a steady rise in prices, and a steady worsening in the balance of payments and, by comparison with Europe and Japan, there was only fairly slow growth. Thus the traditional weapons seemed to have failed for the traditional purposes.

These traditional purposes were all a matter of demand management. But growth is about supply. Is potential supply a function of demand, or is it something else?

There were two basic theories of growth – the expectations theory and a theory of supply constraints. Expectations theory says that if we can raise the ebullience of businessmen so that they become convinced of more rapid growth, then rapid growth will be achieved. The second theory says that we grow at the pace we do because of difficulties of supply, maybe of labour, or of skills, or of capacity, or of management, or of incentives. These two theories can link up if the major constraint is that of physical capacity. Then, more ebullient expectations will themselves break the capacity bottleneck by higher investment, but in Britain a combination of investment subsidies and exhortation had failed to revive confidence to a sufficiently excited level to raise investment adequately. There was thus a flight from past policies and a search for new ones.

In 1961 many factors came together simultaneously. A new credit squeeze occurred, caused by the same old factor, the balance of payments, with the same old symptoms and the same old results. The odious international comparisons continued. There was a new intellectual interest in French planning. A Brighton conference of the Federation of British Industry led businessmen to urge upon a Tory Government the need for new, and therefore better, economic management, and in particular for a change in emphasis, putting rapid growth as the first priority.

It would, of course, be an over-simplification to suggest that there had been no planning in the fifties in the United Kingdom. The public sector was co-ordinated and the nationalized industries and many, especially the large, private firms all conducted planning exercises, but little or nothing was done to ensure that these plans were consistent with each other or, in particular, that any plans were based upon an informed view of the likely future development of the whole economy. In 1962 came the establishment of the National Economic Development Council and the National Economic Development Office (often together called 'Neddy'). These were to draw up a programme for more rapid economic growth and to study the factors influencing it. This was the first step in the creation of new planning machinery, not fundamentally different from the French. It was based on the combination of the theoretical model and an 'industrial inquiry'. The model involved a mixture of forecasting short-term developments and imposing on the economy some overriding policy objective, for example, a given rate of faster growth of GDP plus balance in the balance of payments. The 'industrial inquiry' consisted of asking a large number of significant firms covering a high proportion of total output what their plans were and asking them also to answer a uniform set of questions about their ability to meet a faster rate of growth.

The Neddy target was 4 per cent growth per annum, a compromise figure between the expectations theory which required something to aim at, and the constraints theory which said one must not be too optimistic. This would accelerate growth and require most industries to expand output at a faster rate, and in particular to accelerate the level of investment and the level of exports. Growth in exports had to increase from 3 per cent per annum to 5 per cent per annum in volume. Thus in the most important area of all, the programme was, if anything, the least realistic without specific measures.

In 1964 came a change of government, the creation of the Department of Economic Affairs to take over the planning work of Neddy and a number of other operations as well. The target rate of growth was slightly lowered – from 4 per cent per annum for 1961-66, with an actual rate of 3 per cent, to 3·8 per cent per annum for 1964-70. An atmosphere of great expectations, the need for great speed, and a critical external situation conditioned both the plan and its presentation, and the atmosphere in which it was received. No alternative target rates could be explored and no path could be spelt out of the method of achieving the target rate of growth. We had a detailed picture of what the economy would, or could, be like in 1970 but too little discussion of the path to 1970. We had, as it were, a street map of an unfamiliar city, but no route-map of how to get to it. In particular there was the great difficulty of welding the short-term to the medium-term in the year of 1967, when the required growth of exports plus the required growth of investment meant no room for any growth in consumption, even though incomes would be rising faster than ever before in history. Secondly, the external situation was untenable at the existing exchange rate, but the exchange rate could not be discussed and further external measures could not be outlined.

The procedure was very similar to that of the Neddy plan with a questionnaire to industry, and great econometric calculations to investigate the implications of the faster rate of growth implied in the plan than had been achieved in the past. These implications were, first, for government policy changes; secondly, for various macro-economic magnitudes, such as savings and public expenditure; and thirdly, for the outputs of a large number of industrial sectors.

The National Plan can be criticized on the grounds:

(*a*) that it was technically incompetent;

(*b*) that it was too optimistic in the target growth-rate which was set;

(*c*) that it was not supported by adequate domestic measures to accelerate the growth-rate of productive potential; or

(*d*) that it was not supported by adequate external measures.

The first I would deny. The second and the third are a matter of judgement. The higher target growth-rate implied an acceleration of the rate of productivity increase from the 2·7 per cent annual rate of 1960-64 to 3·4 per cent per annum. It could be argued that the underlying trend growth-rate was itself accelerating anyway, and that with the greater (hoped for) success of demand management, capital formation would grow at a faster and steadier rate. This would combine with micro-economic intervention, outlined and co-ordinated through the score of Economic Development Committees (or 'little Neddies') working in each major industry or sector. These measures aimed at import-saving, export promotion, standardization of output, rationalization of industrial structure, and increased co-operation by the exchange of information. All these measures and their results, whether causal of faster growth or merely permissive, take time, although they are doubtless cumulative. But whether these measures were adequate or not is only a historical point. There is an equally important technical question. What, if any, was the connection between these measures and the National Plan? It is true that the plan would have made no sense without the measures. The converse was not true. Many of them ante-dated the plan, and many of them survived it. But in particular, their effects could not be or were not quantified, nor was their extent or nature altered as a result of any calculations in the plan.

The fourth criticism is both fundamental and inconclusive. It is fundamental in the sense that the 1966 external crisis and the July measures finally destroyed the macro-economic environment which many regarded as the essential background for the success of the micro-economic measures aimed to accelerate growth. It is also fundamental in that the plan itself, at least as published, did not contain defences against such an external crisis. It is, on the other hand, inconclusive in that we can, as yet, hardly confirm or refute whether the underlying rate of growth would have accelerated enough to reach the target anyway. Thus, even had the external position been comfortable, it was not certain that productivity could be raised fast enough or resources diverted to investment fast enough.

Be that as it may, the resort to domestic deflation in July 1966 effectively destroyed whatever chances of success the National Plan *as such* had.

There were, of course, a great number of supporting measures, both domestic and external, implemented both before, during and after the construction of the plan, and to some degree independent of it. On the external side were controls on overseas investment, restraint of overseas government expenditure, a temporary import charge, and an export rebate of indirect taxation. Domestic measures included introduction of corporation tax and the selective employment tax, a switch to investment grants, increases in redundancy payments, the regional employment premium, the Industrial Reorganisation Corporation's promotion of rationalization and mergers.

But these were, or could be, independent of any planning exercise. They will continue as parts of supply-oriented policies. What was destroyed, or at least gravely weakened, was confidence in the merits or usefulness of planning exercises for the whole economy, with detailed output targets for particular industries.

Instruments

Along with experience of planning the economy have come developments in the economic instruments for managing it. In the *monetary policy* field the most important development is the increasing crudity of the controls which are now based largely on directives to financial institutions but with a growing sophistication in the selectivity with which those controls are used as more and more types of finance are selectively expanded or contracted.

Existing financial institutions have been supplemented with the Industrial Reorganisation Corporation (set up in 1966 with a revolving fund of £150 million of taxpayers' money for the encouragement of mergers in industry) and the Industrial Expansion Bill which gives the government the right to take a permanent stake in the equity, i.e. the ownership, of industry where injection of capital and new management is thought to be productive.

In fiscal policy there is again increasing discrimination within investment stimulation which has been going on now since the early fifties, now with the method of investment grants whereby 20 per cent of investment and plant and machinery in the central areas and 40 per cent in the development areas is paid for by public money. There is thus regional discrimination in the stimulation of investment. There is also discrimination in the employment of labour through the selective employment tax which levies a tax on the use of labour in the services and construction industries and pays a premium, the regional employment premium, in 'the regions' to the employers of manufacturing labour. There is, however, deep suspicion in Whitehall of selectivity because it leads to abuse and is often based on arbitrary distinctions.

Public expenditure is also, of course, part of the plan. Fiscal policy, and expenditure by the nationalized industries and public expenditure in the social field are also now carefully planned within the growth target. This is most important since public expenditure accounts for around 40 per cent of gross domestic product.

Incomes policy has gone through many stages – from the Stafford Cripps freeze of the late forties to the 'three wise men', the 'Council for Productivity Prices and Incomes' of the fifties, to the pay pause of 1961-62 supervised by Chancellor Selwyn Lloyd with the guiding light principle, and as partner to Neddy, the National Incomes Commission or Nicky. The trade unions refused to have anything to do with the latter institution.

The change of government in 1964 led to the Declaration of Intent in December: 'urgent and vigorous action to raise productivity throughout industry and commerce, to keep the increase in aggregate money incomes in line with the increase in real national output, and to maintain a steady price level'. In February 1965, the National Board for Prices and Incomes, with Aubrey Jones in the chair, was set up. Then followed the period of the $3\frac{1}{2}$ per cent norm. In Spring 1966 the government took powers to delay wage and price increases for four months; in July 1966 with the squeeze came the freeze, with the zero norm, and for six months no wage increases were permitted. Then followed the period of severe restraint into the present with compulsory powers given to the government to enforce price decreases or to hold back price and wage increases, with a low norm for income increases and a small number of criteria for exceptions.

Regional policy is taking on a new form from being mainly a welfare exercise to being an economic exercise aimed at both parts of the country, both those that are depressed and those that are overheated. The policy consists partly of prohibitions, in the form of the requirement to get Industrial Development Certificates from the Board of Trade if a firm wishes to establish itself or extend itself in the over-extended areas. But in the rest of the country there are various fiscal stimulants in the form of accelerated depreciation, doubling the investment grants, the regional employment premium and often factory sites at less than market price. The policy seems to be working if measured at least by the differential levels of unemployment in the different regions.

The third 'plan' for the UK published in the sixties is 'The Task Ahead; Economic Assessment to 1972'. As its title implies, it is not a plan, or a set of projections, but an assessment of possibilities, i.e. the minimum likely and maximum likely growth-rates of the UK's GDP over a five-year period. But no assessment is made of which is the more likely. It all depends on policies which are in no way linked with, based on or affected by the 'plan' itself, and on underlying economic factors like the growth of the work force. If the gap between the minimum and the maximum is wide (and cumulated over five years, it looks like an ever-widening 'wedge' rather than a line or even a band, giving a range of uncertainty amounting to a number of percentage points on a GDP of over £35 billion) and if structural relationships are less than highly flexible, no private or public sector decisions can be safely based on such an assessment. As an attempt at 'planning without commitment', it ceases to be planning.

Problems

(a) If planning is a device to co-ordinate policy changes to exploit structural relationships, then this is not too unpredictable. But structural changes themselves are by definition more unpredictable, much more non-economic, and planning must cover both areas.

(b) Must planning be quantitative? Can planning only be quantitative? But can it be only quantitative before econometrics has advanced much further? Or is it just as important to emphasize the qualitative aims such as the structural reorganization of industry, the stimulation of research and development, the expansion of exports?

(c) Should planning be the adoption of a single quantitative objective, for example, a target rate of growth? Or is it rather 'making a reasoned choice among various possible combinations of objectives'? This latter, of course, implies the adoption of policies to achieve the preferred combination. There is no such thing as planning without pain, and planning without policies means no planning. Quantitative programmes are of course just as relevant here in choosing rationally one's combination of aims because the trade-off between competing aims may well have to be a quantitative one.

(d) Finally, the real question is – what is the goal of planning? Is it faster growth? Is this the factor which forces change or do we simply wish to select certain changes out of the total possible number of changes in order to achieve the most desired ones?

Conclusions

The planning episode in the UK was expensive. A great deal of time and energy, much discussion, indeed many very expensive man-hours were spent. The opportunity costs were high. In addition, it can be argued that the whole planning exercise distracted policy-makers into a grandiose fatuity, away from sensible but unspectacular influence on other officials, ministers, policies and events.

It arose out of disappointment. In the past, UK economic policy has been driven by successive disappointments to flirt with one novelty after another. This was so in the early fifties with the abandonment of direct controls in favour of a flexible domestic monetary policy (and, very nearly, a flexible exchange rate). Then in the late fifties came further disappointments, and a flirtation with indicative planning. But this was not integrated with policies and, in particular, the urgent triumphed as always over the important. In the UK context, and given the choice of priorities by successive governments, this has meant that the balance of payments and the chosen exchange rate must be protected at all costs – at least at all costs in terms of unemployment and slower growth. It is hard to accelerate actual or even potential growth of supply (the main objective of planning) when the actual growth of demand is severely curtailed.

We are now left with scepticism at best and cynicism at worst; a policy of pragmatism or playing it by ear; endless unco-ordinated tinkering; and a new flirtation with monetary policy. The new planning document of 1969 is so 'open' in the possible alternative outcomes that it offers no guidance to public or private sectors. How can such a wide range of possibilities be 'indicative' of anything to any decision maker? If then planning means 'the premeditated co-ordination of interventions', planning in the UK is dead.

INDEX